The
Historic
Churches
of
Prince
Edward
Island

The Historic Churches of Prince Edward Island

UPDATED 2ND EDITION

H.M. Scott Smith

SSP PUBLICATIONS

National Library of Canada Cataloguing in Publication

Smith, H. M. Scott, 1944-
 The historic churches of Prince Edward Island /
H.M. Scott Smith. — 2nd ed.

(The historic architecture of PEI 1)
Includes bibliographical references and index.
ISBN 0-9686803-8-0

1. Church architecture—Prince Edward Island—History.
2. Churches—Prince Edward Island—History. 3. Church
architecture—Prince Edward Island—Guidebooks.
4. Churches—Prince Edward Island—Guidebooks.
I. Title. II. Series: Historic architecture of PEI 1.

NA5246.P7S64 2004   726.5'09717   C2004-900297-X

Copyright©2004 by H.M. Scott Smith

All rights reserved. No part of this publication may be reproduced, transmitted in any form or by any means– electronic, mechanical, photocopying, display on Internet, recording, stored in a retrieval system, or otherwise, without the prior written consent of the copyright holder. Such use would be infringement of the copyright law. The request of such consent is waived in the case of the reviewer for inclusion in a magazine or newspaper. In such cases, please forward a copy of the publication with this information to H.M. Scott Smith, Box 2472, Halifax, Nova Scotia, B3J 3E4.

Originally published in 1986 by The Boston Mills Press.
Reprinted in 1994 by Stoddart Publishing Co. Ltd.

An SSP Publications Book
Box 2472
Halifax, NS
Canada B3J 3E4
(902) 429-2640

Designed by Gill Stead, Gwen North
Printed in Canada

American Association
for State and Local History
Award of Merit

Winner of the
Heritage Canada
Communications Award

Winner of the
Prince Edward Island
Museum & Heritage Foundation
Publishing Award 1987

FRONT COVER PHOTO:
St. Mary's Roman Catholic Church, Indian River   – Lionel Stevenson

BACK COVER PHOTO:
Interior, St. Patrick's Roman Catholic Church, Fort Augustus – Scott Smith

OVERLEAF: *New Glasgow United Church (1840).*   – Lionel Stevenson

Dedication

This book is dedicated to the memory of G. Edward MacFarlane (1943-1983), a colleague and classmate, whose thoughtfulness, integrity and good cheer were an inspiration to me.

Lancet window detail, St. John's Anglican Church, Ellerslie.
— Lionel Stevenson

Table of Contents

Acknowledgements, 8
Foreword, 9
Introduction, 11
The Religious Context, 13
Built Forms – Early Beginnings, 15
         – The Anglicans
           and the Meeting House, 17
         – The Romantic Movement, 20
Architects and Builders, 26
Construction, 30
Colour Plates, 37
The Historic Churches of
    Prince Edward Island, 49
Location and Index of Churches, 50
Glossary, 121
Period Styles, 125
Selected Bibliography, 127
General Bibliography, 129
About the Author, 131
Index of Churches, 132

Acknowledgements

In the course of preparing this book I have been impressed with similarities to the process of putting a building together – the overall design aspect and attention to details, the structural stability, unity and functions of its various parts. It has also been necessary to implement the team approach much like in an architect's office. I will be eternally grateful to researchers Wendy Duff, Faye Pound and Yvonne Pigott for diligently pursuing a sometimes elusive goal. Only they can appreciate the sheer terror of having to drive a car and examine roadside buildings simultaneously.

A great deal of credit must go to my principal photographer, Lionel Stevenson, who with minimal guidance or suggestion, has managed to capture the essence of Island architecture within both the cultural and physical landscapes. His photographs are stunningly clear and poignant recreations that seem to take us back, etching in our memory timeless images of the Island's proud building heritage. I would also like to mention the fine photographs of Lawrence McLagan, of selected churches in Charlottetown. Other photographic sources are credited individually.

In books of this kind the editorial process can sometimes be as arduous as the actual writing of the text, particularly for the fledgeling historian. I would like to thank the following individuals for their editorial help: Father F.P. Bolger, of the University of Prince Edward Island; Laurie Brinklow of Ragweed Press; Dr. Ken MacKinnon of St. Mary's University, Halifax, Nova Scotia; Elizabeth Pacey; Reg Porter, of the Prince Edward Island Museum and Heritage Foundation; Ian Ross Robertson of the University of Toronto; Anne Hale of Parks Canada; Ed Lindgren; and Archdeacon Robert C. Tuck.

I am grateful to Greg Cook of the Writer's Federation of Nova Scotia, Libby Oughton of Ragweed Press, and Reshard Gool for their encouragement and advice along the way. Draughtsman Gerard McMahon and typist Faye Smith deserve a lot of credit for somehow deciphering my tiny scribbles. Many thanks to designer Gill Stead for a job well done, and to the Denisons at Boston Mills Press, thanks for your patience, tea and doughnuts.

Finally I would be totally remiss if I did not acknowledge the financial assistance of the Canada Council's Explorations Program, the Department of the Secretary of State, the Prince Edward Island Council of the Arts, and the Nova Scotia Department of Culture, Recreation and Fitness.

Foreword

This book was born in July of 1978 when I began an investigation into the origins of Prince Edward Island architecture. Documentation of the Island's historic architecture to that point had been minimal beyond the Canadian Inventory of Historic Buildings and the efforts of a few individuals. I conducted a superficial survey of all building types in Prince Edward Island, and then journeyed to southern England, Ireland, the Highlands and Hebrides of Scotland, and the New England region of the United States in an attempt to establish the complex correlations between Prince Edward Island buildings and their antecedents. I then selected particular Island buildings for further study, based on the following parameters:
1) built before 1914;
2) a substantial and/or relevant architectural form;
3) associated with a significant historical event or personality;
4) in good physical repair and as faithful as possible to its original state.

The result will be four distinct catalogues of architecturally and historically significant pre-World War I buildings in Prince Edward Island, with brief insights into their origins. This first book on churches will be followed in succession by volumes on houses, the buildings associated with agriculture and the fishery, and public buildings.

During the course of my investigations, I learned many things beyond the more obvious architectural conclusions. I have learned what it is that makes Prince Edward Island architecture unique – the forethought and practicality of the pioneer builders that placed decoration in a symbolic role in the context of an economic style. Lines are clean and straight with precious little wasted space and few superfluous elements. The rolling topography and the extreme coastal climate, with heavy precipitation and high winds have made it necessary for Island builders to look for shelter – the lee side of a hill, a protected harbour or a windbreak of trees. The idyllic postcard scene of a pastoral Island farm often does not reveal the strategy behind the building's situation.

In observing photographers Stevenson and McLagan, I have learned much about the photography of buildings and indirectly, the visual aspects of architecture. They have taught me a different way to "see" buildings objectively, from all aspects, and that motion and haste are not conducive to a deeper appreciation of the "Queen of the Arts".

Perhaps the most significant lesson that I have learned relates to people — the hardy and resourceful generations of Scots, Irish, English and Acadians who carved communities out of the wilderness because they had a will to. This resolute adherence to the principles of practical and functional architecture, from one generation to the next, has been a profound revelation to me. These are also the people who have welcomed this inquisitive stranger into their homes. May I apologize in advance for any errors, omissions, misinterpretations, inaccurate dates or misspellings of proper names.

Economic prosperity is well known as the enemy of architectural conservation in that it promotes new construction. In this period of relative prosperity in Prince Edward Island, the stock of historic buildings is gradually dwindling. Although Prince Edward Island is quite advanced in the area of conservation awareness, it is most urgent that all responsible heritage organizations and agencies adopt policies of inventory and education rather than legislation in order to preserve the integrity and promote sympathetic re-use of those buildings threatened with destruction or decay. Not intended as a history text or a manual of preservation, I sincerely hope that this book and its successors will prove to be useful tools in this conservation effort. To this end, I have adopted a subjective but uncritical stance in the hope that the information contained herein will be accessible and enjoyable to everyone.

Scott Smith
Halifax, January 2004

Church of Scotland, Dunvegan, Isle of Skye, Scotland. – Scott Smith

Introduction

CHURCH BUILDINGS HAVE long been a vital cultural signpost in Island communities. They are among the most significant and, in many cases, the longest surviving representatives of a community's religious aspirations and social and cultural values. For most settlers, the church served as a source of strength and refuge from the rigours of pioneer life, and for this reason the first church buildings are often the most enduring of testimonials to the skill of the immigrant builders.

The early settlers in Prince Edward Island — the Acadians, Scots, Loyalists, English and Irish — had to contend with vastly different geographical and climatic conditions from those of their homelands. Where they used to build in stone, they now had to build in wood, and the constraints of their passage to the New Land left them relatively restricted in terms of tools. They did, however, bring with them something essential: the inspiration of an architectural form derived from church buildings in their home-

St. Augustine's Roman Catholic Church, South Rustico. — Lionel Stevenson

lands. They built modest and simplified versions of the churches they had previously known. Adjustments, refinements and, sometimes, by necessity, compromises had to be made. Ultimately, the results were well-suited to their new context.

The spiritual aspirations of the Island's pioneers were manifested in a distinct building form. In the early communities the church evolved as the most ornate and substantial of all the buildings, and, as such, became the dominant architectural form. In the lush, rolling Prince Edward Island landscape, and in contrast to the other more utilitarian buildings, the church stands out as a fine jewel. *(see pages 41, 48)*

What follows is a brief analysis of the social and architectural factors that determined the size, form and character of the Island's churches. It is necessary to introduce some of the men who designed and built these churches, as well as some of the techniques they used. The final section is a collection of profiles of the most historically and architecturally significant pre-1914 churches in Prince Edward Island.

The Religious Context

The first organized ecclesiastical missions in Prince Edward Island were established by the Acadians after the year 1720. Over the course of the previous century their Roman Catholicism had taken root with the establishment of the marshland communities of the Bay of Fundy region of New Brunswick and Nova Scotia. After the Treaty of Paris was signed in 1763, thereby ceding most French possessions in North America to Great Britain, the Church of England began to assume a dominant role, particularly in the Island's capital city, Charlottetown. Reverend Theophilus DesBrisay was the first rector appointed, in 1774, and St. Paul's Church in Charlottetown (1801) became the focal point of Anglicanism in the province.

Through legislation and restrictive land grants, the Protestant government officials suppressed the growth of the Roman Catholic Church for more than half a century. Nevertheless, a steady influx of Roman Catholic immigrants continued, principally from southern Ireland and the Catholic areas of the Scottish Highlands. Reverend James MacDonald, himself a Scottish immigrant, ministered faithfully to his scattered flock of Scots and Acadian French from 1772 to 1785.

The Protestant dominance was further reinforced by the arrival of the Loyalists and Lowland Scots, beginning in 1783. Although the Loyalists were almost all adherents of the Church of England, there were some non-conformists among them, who belonged to sects that preferred a separate existence for their church, independent of the state-supported Church of England. The arrival of Congregationalists, Methodists, Baptists and Presbyterians effectively strengthened and diversified the Protestant majority.

Benjamin Chappell introduced Methodism to Prince Edward Island in 1775. Chappell was an immigrant from London, England, and a personal friend of John Wesley. He settled in the New London area of the Island's north shore, but moved to Charlottetown in 1778. Due to his influence, most Methodists on the island were Wesleyans, with the exception of a small group of Bible Christians. Almost all Methodists emigrated directly from England, and by 1850 had established a significant foothold on the Island.

The revival that led to the establishment of the Baptist faith in the Maritimes was brought about by Henry Alline, the famous "New Light" preacher from Nova Scotia. Alline visited the Island in 1782 and "the word" was quickly spread by such lay preachers as John Scott, Alexander Crawford and Dr. John Knox. Most Baptists were Loyalists or immigrants from Nova Scotia or New Brunswick; however a community of "Scotch Baptists" was established at Cross Roads in the early 1800s. This congregation later seceded from the Baptist Church to found one of the earliest Disciples of Christ churches in Canada.

With the late eighteenth-century arrival of the Loyalists and Highland Scots came Presbyterianism. The roots of this religion were planted firmly in the Calvinism expounded by

Scotland's John Knox. Reverend James McGregor was the earliest Presbyterian missionary to visit, in 1791, and Reverend John Urquhart and Reverend Dr. John Keir were instrumental in establishing the Church of Scotland in the Malpeque-New London area. In the mid-1800s, the Presbyterian Church began foreign missionary work in the south Pacific, and the Reverends John Geddie and George Gordon gave their lives to this cause. Men like MacGregor, Keir and Geddie belonged to the independent, or secessionist, branch of the Presbyterian tradition.

The established, or state, Church of Scotland produced one of the most colourful and influential figures in the religious history of Prince Edward Island. Reverend Donald McDonald created a semi-independent body of some five thousand followers within the Church of Scotland on the Island. His group, commonly known as the "McDonaldites," was scattered over the thirteen congregations which he served on an itinerant basis. "The Minister," as he was known to his people, possessed unbounded zeal and charisma and attracted his following by the force of his highly animated style of preaching.

In the 1850's, the ratio of Protestants to Roman Catholics had been reduced to 55:45, with the Roman Catholic church firmly entrenched, particularly in rural towns and villages. The emancipation of the Roman Catholics in Prince Edward Island was due in large measure to the efforts and dedication of the missionary priest, Reverend Angus Bernard MacEachern, who ministered to his widely dispersed subjects between the years 1790 and 1835. In 1829 he was appointed the first Bishop of Charlottetown,

Victoria United Church, Victoria. Originally a Wesleyan Methodist church, built in 1877. — Lionel Stevenson

and he and his successor, Reverend Bernard Donald MacDonald, were instrumental in acquiring a status of equality for the Roman Catholic Church on the Island.

By the late nineteenth century, a number of attempts were made within Canadian Protestant ranks to achieve interdenominational harmony and even unity. The result of these efforts was the historic 1925 merger of Methodists, Congregationalists and some Presbyterian congregations to form the United Church of Canada.

Reconstruction of Acadian chapel at Mt. Carmel. – Scott Smith

Built Forms
Early Beginnings

The earliest organized religious gatherings in Prince Edward Island were held in private homes. These meetings were presided over by itinerant ministers or priests who logged many miles over primitive cart paths on foot, horseback or in horse-drawn buggies to reach their destinations. Sometimes they had to cross bodies of water in open boats and there are accounts of arduous, wintry ice passages. These courageous and dedicated preachers visited the fledgling communities as infrequently as once every six months.

It was not until the late eighteenth and early nineteenth centuries that the first church buildings were erected; these were small, primitive log structures which often served more than one denomination. They were temporary buildings that deteriorated quickly, and virtually no trace of them exists today. The Acadians built simple frame churches, usually of vertical *piquets* or horizontal *pièces sur pièces* construction. The cracks between the logs were often filled with a mixture of clay and straw (*colombage bousillée*) and the roof was often thatched. Unfortunately, these

15

tiny chapels were destroyed by the British shortly after the Expulsion of the Acadians in 1758. All of these early churches were extremely crude, with dirt floors, few windows, inadequate ventilation and simple log or plank seats. Some of the earliest Roman Catholic churches also had log or plank altars and handcarved crucifixes.

These humble buildings often functioned as meeting halls and schoolhouses, and, as such, became the social and cultural centres of the emerging communities. For this reason, they were given a place of prominence, strategically located on the highest point of land and situated with their longitudinal axis usually in the east-west direction. It was not until the second quarter of the nineteenth century that separate schoolhouses and meeting halls were built, along with larger and more substantial churches.

Corner detail, church reconstruction at Selkirk settlement, Island Market Village, North River.
– Scott Smith

Built Forms
The Anglicans and the Meeting House

In proportion and form, some of the smaller Anglican parish churches built in the Atlantic region in the late eighteenth and early nineteenth centuries were reduced versions of St. Paul's Anglican Church in Halifax, Nova Scotia. Based on James Gibbs' Marylbone Chapel (St. Peter's, Vere Street) in London, England, St. Paul's was built in 1750 in the neo-Classic, Palladian Style. The detailing of other Anglican churches in the region was also neo-Classic — the inspiration from the Old World being realized more through the minor elements of design than through imitation of the church as a whole. By early in the nineteenth century, however, Gothic details were beginning to appear, particularly in the cities and towns. Pointed Gothic window forms and tracery, quatrefoils, mouldings and decorative wooden ceilings were really forerunners of the pervasive Gothic Revival that was to follow. The Anglican churches of this period in Prince Edward Island were caricatures of their more formal predecessor, the English Gothic church. St. John's Anglican Church in St. Eleanor's is a good example *(see page 102)*. Built in 1825, destroyed by fire in 1835 and rebuilt in 1838, it is the oldest extant Anglican church in the province.

St. Paul's Anglican Church, Halifax, Nova Scotia (1750).
— Scott Smith

The migrations of New Englanders to the Maritime provinces that began in 1760 and continued through the Loyalist influx of 1783-1785 included the non-conformist denominations mentioned earlier. They imported a new church

Barrington meeting-house, Barrington, Nova Scotia (1765).
— Nova Scotia Government Services

form called the "meeting house" — a combination of English parish church and English town hall that originated with the Puritans. Bishop John Medley described it thus:

> "The ordinary type seems to have been borrowed from the buildings erected by the Puritans... the Church having no form of its own, not having apparently any reference to the ancient churches in the other country....
> Happily the greater part of these edifices were built of wood, and must ere long decay."

The meeting house was based on the architecture of religious dissent developed in New England by the Congregationalists: a multipurpose assembly hall, with the pulpit located on a side wall of the nave and the chancel eliminated in order to bring the preacher closer to the con-

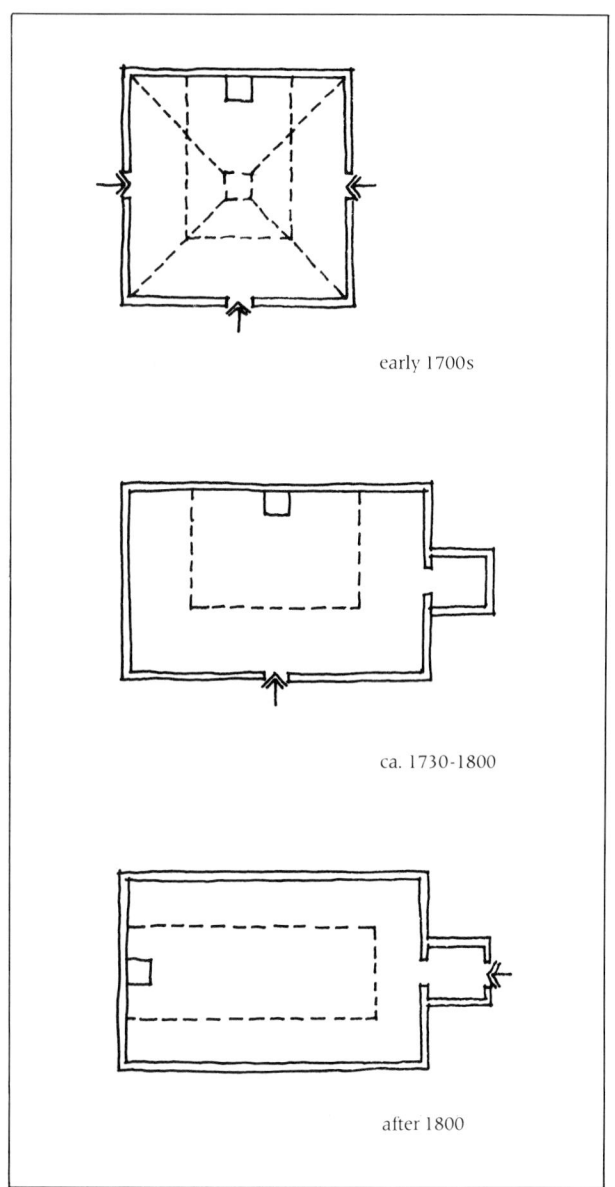

Evolution of the meeting-house plan.
— courtesy George Rogers

Interior, Free Church of Scotland, Desable. — Lionel Stevenson

gregation. The pews surrounded the pulpit on three sides and many meeting houses had a three-sided gallery above. The plan was square and simple, reflecting the building's dual role. The interiors were very austere, with little or no colour or decoration. Timber-framed and covered with clapboard or shingle, the meeting house was a direct response to local conditions by the Congregationalists and other denominations that built them. The detailing of these early meeting houses was initially neo-Classic, but in the early 1800s Gothic features began to appear. Today on the Island, we most often find a combination of the two.

In Prince Edward Island, the meeting house form was adopted by other non-Anglican protestant denominations in addition to the Congregationalists — the Baptists, Presbyterians and Methodists for example — but by early in the nineteenth century, some of these denominations had begun to assimilate. The meeting house form began to change, to become "churchified." Physically, the proportions of the plan became more elongated, a bell tower was added at one end of the nave and the pulpit shifted to the opposite end. The early hipped roof gave way to a gabled roof and more ornamentation began to appear. The social hierarchy in the seating arrangement gradually disappeared. The meeting house had become a place for religious purposes alone.

The hybrid church form of the early nineteenth century was really the beginning of a Maritime vernacular church architecture; the trappings of British neo-Classic and/or neo-Gothic details superimposed on eighteenth century meeting house structures. Some good examples of the meeting house genre in Prince Edward Island are the Free Church of Scotland at Desable, the Geddie Memorial Church at Springbrook, the First Baptist Church at Cross Roads (Cross Roads Christian Church) and St. James United Church at West Covehead.

Built Forms
The Romantic Movement

Emigration from Britain to the Atlantic region in the late eighteenth and early nineteenth centuries brought with it a new attitude toward architecture. It became a priority to promote images of stability and strength, an expression of confidence in the emerging British Empire in the New World. For this reason, North American architects and builders turned to the symbolism of the Classic Revival as a stylistic model for their public buildings. Roman Neoclassicism was derived from the work of the writer and architect Vitruvius and subsequently the Italian architect Palladio. While Classicism was imported to England in the seventeenth century by Inigo Jones, Palladianism was applied in Britain in the eighteenth century by Sir Christopher Wren and a Scot named James Gibbs.

The Classic Revival was not universally adopted in eastern Canada and was confined almost exclusively to the design of public buildings. Such architects as John Plaw and Isaac Smith did work in this style in Prince Edward Island. The most impressive example of a Palladian Classic Revival building is Province House in Charlottetown, completed in 1847. Elements of the style — pilasters, eave returns, pediments and round-headed windows — were evident in the detailing of smaller Protestant church buildings up until the mid-nineteenth century. St. James United Church at West Covehead is a good example of the application of Classic Revival embellishment to a rural Protestant church.

The Gothic Revival which followed more truly provided nineteenth-century North Americans with a picturesque reflection of their northern European cultural tradition. This decorated, irregular style evolved through several phases between 1830 and 1900, and dominated the design of church buildings in Prince Edward Island — and indeed most of urban North America — throughout this period. So pervasive was this style that even smaller rural churches were built in modest interpretations of the Gothic Revival known as the Carpenter-Gothic or Picturesque Styles. By the end of the nineteenth century, most denominations had embraced either the French or English Gothic Revival as the correct style for their churches.

Gothic architecture originated in medieval France and England in the twelfth and thirteenth centuries respectively. It superseded a Norman Style that, with few exceptions such as the cathedrals at Durham and Saint-Denis, was relatively severe and horizontal. The Gothic Style developed in a series of phases through the Tudor Style of the sixteenth century, but the characteristics of the Victorian Gothic Revival can more accurately be traced to the zenith of its development: the Decorated and Perpendicular Phases of the fourteenth century in England and the Flamboyant Phase in France.

The French and English Gothic Revivals differed in aspects of stylistic purity. The English Revival, as promoted by the Ecclesiologists, favoured a clean and pure interpretation of the

Gothic vocabulary. The French Revival movement was more divergent, incorporating shallower transepts, apsidal, or octagonal chancel walls, a unified massing of nave and chancel, and, in a later stage, an asymmetrically located tower.

The groin vaulting, with its elaborate fans and ribs, the flying buttresses, decorated columns and mouldings, the pointed arches and windows with their delicate tracery and the soaring towers and spires were design elements that emphasized the vertical. These formed the physical vocabulary of the Gothic Revival which reached North America in the early nineteenth century, largely through the influence of the Cambridge Camden Society (later named the Ecclesiological Society) and such English architects as James Wyatt, A.W. Pugin and William Butterfield. They greatly influenced the work of such American architects as Richard Upjohn, John Notman, Robert Long Jr. and J.W. Priest. Publications such as "The Ecclesiologist" and the writings of Pugin, Upjohn, A.J. Downing and A.J. Davis were instrumental in establishing the Gothic spirit in North America.

Although the Gothic Revival was alive and well in Canada in the mid-nineteenth century, the Gothic embellishments of Maritime churches were just a hint of the grand revival to follow. It really began in Quebec with the construction of the controversial Church of Notre-Dame in Montreal. A Georgian body clad in Gothic dress, the church was designed by an Irish New Yorker, James O'Donnell, and completed in 1829. Although Ontario and western Canada were initially not as receptive to the Gothic Revival movement, William Thomas was a major proponent of the earlier English Gothic Style; he built several churches in this style, mostly in Ontario, in the mid-nineteenth century.

St. John's Anglican Church in Saint John, New Brunswick incorporates many elements of the Gothic Revival Style. Also known as the Stone Church, it is probably the earliest church built of stone in the region. Begun in 1824, it was designed by local architect Lloyd Johnston. It was not, however, until about twenty years later that two churches were built that were destined to have the greatest impact on church design and construction in the Atlantic provinces. St. John the Baptist Anglican Cathedral in St. John's, Newfoundland, dates from 1843. English architect George Gilbert Scott was later commissioned to rebuild this church in a modified Gothic Revival Style shortly after a devastating fire had razed it to the ground in 1846. Christ Church Cathedral in Fredericton, New Brunswick, is pure Gothic; its design is essentially a copy of a late thirteenth-century English parish church, St. Mary's Church in Snettisham, Norfolk. Built between 1846 and 1853, Christ Church Cathedral is the inspiration of Bishop John Medley, and its purity can be attributed to the influence of the Ecclesiological Society. Designed by architects Frank Wills and William Butterfield, Christ Church Cathedral and the exquisite St. Anne's Chapel (1846) nearby established a precedent in pure Gothic design in the region for the next half-century. Maritime architects, including William Harris of Prince Edward Island, looked to them and to Quebec for inspiration. The challenge remained for these architects to transpose the stylistic elements of the Gothic Revival from stone into wood.

St. Mary's Anglican Church, Summerside. — Scott Smith

Princetown United Church, Malpeque, before addition of new spire in July, 1984. — Lionel Stevenson

Catholic Church in Tignish (1860), constructed of brick, and St. Mary's Roman Catholic Church at Indian River (1902) built of wood, are all excellent interpretations of the Gothic Revival Style.

Charlottetown, the capital city of Prince Edward Island, has long been the centre of Anglicanism in the province. It is there too that we find the largest Protestant churches. St. Peter's Cathedral (1869) and St. Paul's Anglican Church (1895) exemplify the High Victorian Gothic Revival idiom. St. John's Anglican Church in Milton (1898) is a smaller frame church built in the French Gothic Style. St. Mary's Anglican Church in Summerside (1907) is a handsome brick church designed by architect George Baker.

The pastoral countryside of Prince Edward Island is dotted with seemingly countless little white churches built in the Picturesque or Carpenter-Gothic Style. The United Church at Malpeque and St. John's Anglican Church in Ellerslie typify this popular style of church.

There is some evidence of further stylistic development in church architecture on the Island, beyond the Gothic Revival up until the beginning of the First World War. The design of the

St. James Roman Catholic Church, Summerfield.
– Lionel Stevenson

Central Christian Church, Charlottetown.
– Lawrence McLagan

Church of Christ in Montague (1876) embodies elements of the Italianate Style, and Central Christian Church in Charlottetown (1900) has a round Château Style tower. The eclectic Sacred Heart Roman Catholic Church at Mount Ryan (Johnston's River), built in 1916, is essentially Spanish Revival in style. St. James Roman Catholic Church in Summerfield, built in 1928, is an interesting combination of Baroque, neo-Classic and Italianate elements.

While there was not a proliferation of what could be called an indigenous style, local builders certainly left their mark on such churches as St. John's Presbyterian Church in Belfast, Cascumpec United Church (1872) and St. John's Anglican Church in Ellerslie. Little Sands United Church (1898) is a rare example of a purely indigenous church style.

William Critchlow Harris at age 28 years. A painting by his brother Robert Harris.
– Confederation Centre of the Arts, Charlottetown

Architects and Builders

The role of the architect in church construction in Prince Edward Island became more pronounced during the latter half of the nineteenth century. Earlier master builders and highly skilled carpenters were responsible for what were sometimes unique interpretations of the Gothic Revival idiom. An example of this is St. John's Presbyterian Church at Belfast, built by Robert Jones. In the latter part of the nineteenth century, the Roman Catholic Church underwent a period of growth and expansion on the Island and several large rural churches were either constructed or rebuilt. Architects such as Thomas Alley, Charles Chappell, John McLellan, John Corbett, John Hunter, George Baker, David Stirling, F-X.E. Meloche, and R.P. Lemay were quite active at this time, but it was William Critchlow Harris who left the greatest between 1880 and 1913. Twenty of these were new churches or church renovations in Prince Edward Island, sixteen of which are still standing. His interpretation of the High Victorian Gothic Revival vocabulary, although not particularly adventurous, is unmistakable throughout the Island, and indeed the Maritime, landscape.

Harris studied the models in Fredericton and Quebec closely and his conservative, provincial approach to the High Victorian Gothic Revival idiom may well have contributed to his greatest disappointment: the loss of the commission to design All Saints Cathedral in Halifax. Nonetheless, Harris' contributions to regional ecclesiastical architecture are substantial, including his adaptation of the Gothic Revival Style for the designs of smaller Protestant churches such as St. John's Anglican Church at Milton and the renovation of St. Elizabeth's Anglican Church at Springfield. Unfortunately, one of his most charming interpretations of the Carpenter-Gothic Style, St. Thomas's Anglican Church at Long Creek, has been converted into a summer cottage.

Harris also steadfastly promoted the use of local sandstone in the construction of some of his churches. The beautiful reddish hue of the stone dramatically enhanced the monumentality of the Gothic Revival Style. He was also a tasteful and meticulous designer of interiors, as the soaring, groined ceilings of St. Patrick's Roman Catholic Church in Fort Augustus and the exquisite All Souls' Chapel in Charlottetown attest. An amateur musician, Harris painstakingly calculated the acoustics of his churches to respond in much the same way that a musical instrument might. He applied these principles to St. Paul's Anglican Church in Charlottetown

St. Elizabeth's Anglican Church, Springfield. – Lionel Stevenson

legacy of High Victorian Gothic Revival churches.

William Harris was born in Liverpool, England, in 1854, and at the age of two immigrated with his family to Charlottetown. Harris apprenticed in Halifax with architect David Stirling, who taught him the fundamentals of the early Gothic Revival. During his career, Harris designed or contributed to the design of some 120 buildings

27

Interior, St. Malachy's Roman Catholic Church, Kinkora. — Lionel Stevenson

and to later churches with, for the most part, outstanding results.

Recent renovations to some of his churches may have tarnished some of Harris' Gothic dreams, but St. Mary's Roman Catholic Church at Indian River — although faced with a somewhat uncertain future — still stands as an excellent example of his attention to detail and acoustics. It exemplifies the success with which he adapted a relatively flamboyant urban style to a large timber-frame rural church.

Although perhaps not blessed with the artistry of his brother Robert Harris, a renowned portrait painter, William Harris was an architect of considerable dimension. He possessed a particular perception of, and sensibility to, the architec-

Winding stair to gallery, St. Mary's Roman Catholic Church, Indian River. Hexagonal motif in flooring is a repetitive element throughout the church. — Lionel Stevenson

tural and cultural conditions of his own time and place. His excellent watercolour renderings of his own projects, many of which were built in Nova Scotia or not built at all, exist to this day in the vaults of the Confederation Centre art gallery in Charlottetown. *(see page 42)*

Although more and more architects became involved in church design after 1850, their drawings did not contain much more detail than a set of today's conceptual drawings. The onus was clearly on the builders and master carpenters to follow through on the architects' designs. Fortunately, Prince Edward Island was blessed with an abundance of these highly skilled builders, such as George Tanton, Wilfred Maynard, Harry Williams, George Gard, Bernard Creamer, and Nathan MacFarlane. They not only mastered wood construction techniques, but also developed a fine sense of design and detail. In churches without side-aisles, the longer spans necessitated timber roof framing that was uncommonly sophisticated for the period. The complexities of framing the groin vaulted ceilings of Harris' churches can well be imagined.

Shingle detail, East Point United Baptist Church
– Lionel Stevenson

Construction

The construction of early church buildings in Prince Edward Island was executed initially in log and later almost exclusively in timber frame. The task of building churches presented some new problems for the resourceful pioneer builders. Floors had to be reinforced to support the extra weight of the congregation, and clear vision to the pulpit became imperative. This was solved by spanning the nave with roof trusses, which sometimes received intermediate support from extended gallery posts.

Among the Loyalists were some highly skilled carpenters and joiners who used barn construction techniques in building their early churches. Frames were cut and assembled on the ground and raised onto sandstone foundations during the celebrated "raising bee," an event that was a practical and efficient method of erection, as well as a joyous social occasion. The joints were frequently mortise-and-tenon, reinforced with wooden pegs. Later, emigration from the south of England brought skilled ship's carpenters to

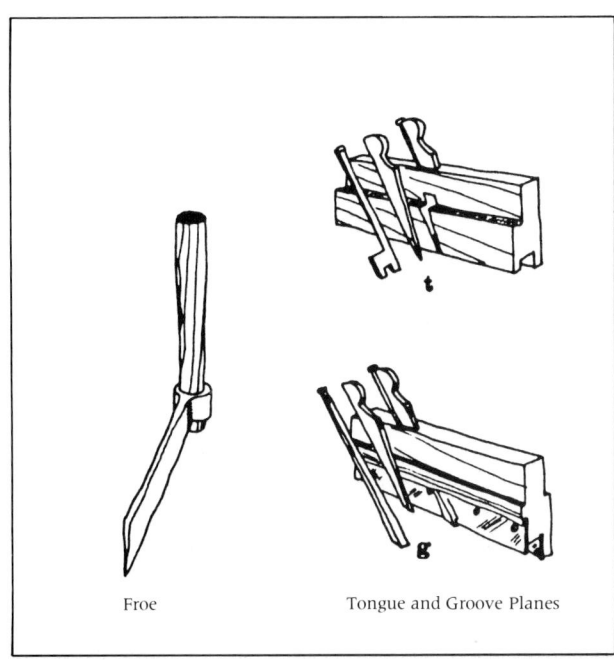

Froe Tongue and Groove Planes

– courtesy George Rogers

Charlottetown, Summerside and the Port Hill area. They introduced bracing known as "ship's knees" and roof framing that was similar to that of an inverted ship's hull. In fact, the term "nave" is derived from the Latin "navis," meaning ship.

Pioneer church builders were quite ingenious in their adaptation to the new environment. Walls were insulated with sawdust, seaweed or brick nogging, and birch bark was sometimes used as a moisture barrier. Exteriors were clad either in clapboard, the refined New England successor to the English weather-boarding system, or shingles cut locally. Vertical board-and-batten siding became quite popular after 1840, but St. Mark's Anglican Church in Kensington (1885) is one of the few surviving examples. Until the development of paint, outer walls were coated in a lime whitewash. The interiors were finished either in lath and plaster or a rough board sheathing — vertical or horizontal — often with a wide board wainscoting.

Until the second half of the nineteenth century, when sawmills became quite common on the Island, pit sawing was the method of splitting timber into boards of widths of up to two feet or more. A deep pit was dug in the ground and a tandem of sawyers, one above and the other below, would slice a log down its length with their big cross-cut saw. A variety of woods were used for everything from rough framing members to window frames to church furniture. Pine, oak, fir, poplar, birch, maple, ash or hemlock were the most common varieties, but on occasion more exotic woods such as teak, rosewood, cherry or mahogany were imported to manufacture church furniture, statues or decorative trim.

Pioneer carpenters and joiners placed great value on their tools. They made some themselves, but brought most with them from New England or the Old Country. For rough framing or detailed finishing, tools such as the axe, saw, adze, plane and chisel, and hole-makers such as the awl, auger or gimlet, were vital accessories. New tools were developed in the New Land, such as the frow or "froe," a tool used with a mallet for splitting shingles, lath or clapboard, and the tongue-and-groove plane, used to create a snug joint between boards. The interiors of some of the early Island churches reveal that he pioneer carpenters and joiners had developed their craft to a very high standard.

Later additions to a church, such as a bell tower, vestry or chancel were framed separately and attached to the main frame of the nave with wooden pegs or bolts. The Geddie Memorial Church in Springbrook, however, has a bell tower that was built later and adjacent to the original church. Bell towers were heavily framed and reinforced to carry the extra load of the bell, which sometimes weighed as much as five tons.

In the latter half of the nineteenth century, devastating fires in both Charlottetown and Summerside prompted city officials and church administrators to consider the alternatives of using Island-made brick or native sandstone in the construction of new church buildings. William Harris, as previously noted, was a major proponent of the use of Island sandstone in these later churches, but it was the proliferation of brick kilns throughout the Island during the 1860s and 1870s that provided a competitive, albeit highly controversial, alternative. The brick, it seems, was of questionable quality. St. Patrick's Roman Catholic Church at Fort Augustus was rebuilt in brick after a fire destroyed it in 1897. St. Simon and St. Jude Roman Catholic Church in Tignish (1860), Montague's Church of Christ (1876), St. Joachim's Roman Catholic Church in Vernon River (1877) and Notre-Dame de Mont Carmel Roman Catholic Church in Mont Carmel (1899) are larger churches whose brick walls, for the most part, have withstood the rigours of time and weather. St. Martin's Roman Catholic Church at Cumberland (1868) and South Winsloe United Church (1880) are two smaller rural churches built of sandstone and brick, respectively.

Tower framing, St. John's Presbyterian Church, Belfast.
– Lionel Stevenson

Most of the master masons and stonecarvers who built the Island's stone churches were of Scottish origin, imported to the region with the military or specifically to ply their trade in the New Land. Stone used in church construction was usually red Island sandstone, but freestone

Interior, St. John's United Church, Mount Stewart. (1853) — Scott Smith

from Wallace, Nova Scotia was occasionally imported for some church buildings, most notably St. Dunstan's Basilica in Charlottetown (1919). The local sandstone was in abundant supply. It was soft and porous and easily quarried, but for this reason there was some doubt concerning its structural stability. Sandstone was not the only type of stone used. Granite ballast from visiting ships has been found in some foundations and as decorative and liturgical elements. St. Paul's Roman Catholic Church in Sturgeon (1892), St. Mary's Roman Catholic Church in Souris (1902) (1928) and St. Paul's Anglican Church in Charlottetown (1895) are fine churches built of Island sandstone.

Before the 1930s, an alarming number of Island churches were either destroyed or severely damaged by fire. St. Mary's Roman Catholic

Notre Dame de Mont Carmel Roman Catholic Church (1896-98), Mont Carmel. — Lionel Stevenson

Church at Indian River and St. Mary's Roman Catholic Church at Souris are two larger churches that were totally destroyed and later rebuilt. The stone walls and tower of the original Souris church, however, survived. These fires were caused by lightning strikes, faulty furnaces or flues, or, more recently, inadequate wiring from the early days of electrical power. Several churches have lost their spires, either from light-

ning strikes, fires, neglect or improper structural design. Church Union in 1925 precipitated the renovations of many churches and rendered many more obsolete. As some Presbyterian congregations refused to accept this union, additional churches had to be built to accommodate them. Some redundant buildings were sold and converted into community halls, craft shops or summer cottages, while others were dismantled

Hand-carved figurines of the twelve apostles in niches in the spire. St. Mary's Roman Catholic Church, Indian River. – Lionel Stevenson

altogether. Population shifts, particularly from rural areas to towns and cities, left more than one rural church in a derelict state or for sale. Liturgical changes, most noticeably within the Roman Catholic Church, prompted not only major planning changes, but also more subtle variations in such aspects as altar placement and decoration.

In terms of decoration, the early Protestant churches were rather austere, although St. John's Presbyterian Church in Belfast and St. John's Anglican Church in Ellerslie are exceptions. In general, it was the more affluent Roman Catholic Church that could afford the elaborate windows, reredos, frescoes, statues, groin-vaulted ceilings, clerestories and other functional and decorative elements. These were also a reflection of the more complex Roman Catholic liturgy and their attitude toward the status of the church in the community.

The list of craftsmen who worked on these church interiors is lengthy indeed, and many were imported to perform specialized tasks such as delicate wood carving and masonry detailing. Church furniture, such as altars, fonts, pews, pulpits and organs, was often built elsewhere, usually in Quebec. Artists and sculptors were often commissioned to execute the frescoes, stained glass windows, murals, stencilling, reredos, statues and low relief that adorn most Roman Catholic churches. A trend developed toward the turn of the century in which architects such as William Harris became more involved in the detailed design of the relatively important appointments of the church interior, such as the altar and pulpit, much in the way that Pugin and Butterfield had been earlier.

Chair, St. Bonaventure's Roman Catholic Church, Tracadie Cross.
– Lionel Stevenson

Geddie Memorial Church, Springbrook. — Lionel Stevenson

Column and vaulted ceiling, St. Paul's Anglican Church, Charlottetown.
– Lawrence McLagan

Gallery stair, St. Mary's Roman Catholic Church, Indian River.
– Lionel Stevenson

Interior, St. John's Anglican Church, Ellerslie. — Lionel Stevenson

St. John's Presbyterian Church, Belfast (Pinette). – Scott Smith

Immaculate Conception Roman Catholic Church, Brae. (1903) — Lionel Stevenson

41

Pew detail, St. Mary's Roman Catholic Church, Indian River.
– Lionel Stevenson

Vaulting, Immaculate Conception Roman Catholic Church, Brae. (1903)
– Scott Smith

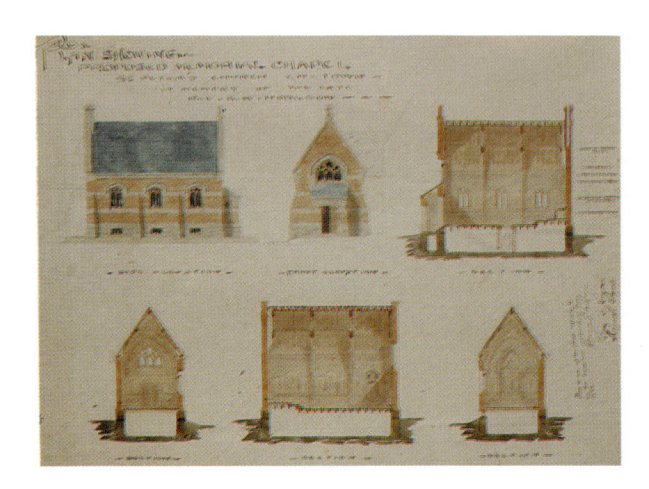

William Critchlow Harris watercolour rendering. All Souls' Chapel.
– Courtesy Keith Pickard

Freize detail from presbytery, St. Patrick's Roman Catholic Church, Fort Augustus.
– Scott Smith

Hartsville Presbyterian Church, Hartsville.

– Scott Smith

Rose Window, St. Dunstan's Basilica, Charlottetown. – Lawrence McLagan

Interior, All Soul's Chapel, St. Peter's Cathedral, Charlottetown.
– Lawrence McLagan

St. Paul's Roman Catholic Church. Sturgeon. – Lionel Stevenson

Holy Trinity Anglican Church, Georgetown. – R.C. Tuck

Interior, Geddie Memorial Church, Springbrook. – Lionel Stevenson

Interior, Free Church of Scotland, Desable. – Lionel Stevenson

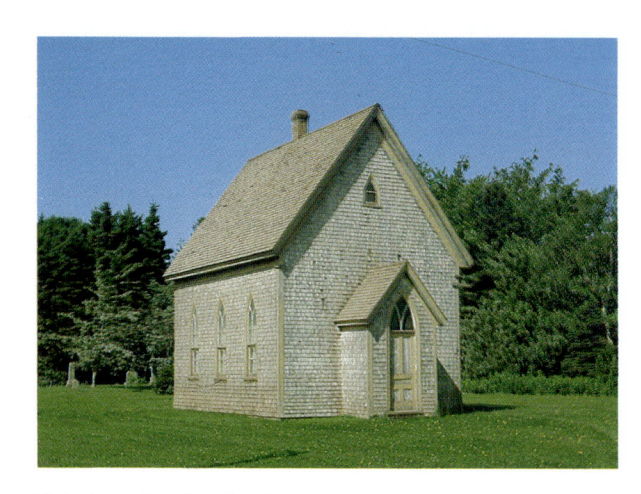

United Baptist Church, Alma. (1908) – Scott Smith

St. Mary's Roman Catholic Church, Indian River. – Lionel Stevenson

Orwell Corner United Church, Orwell Corner. (1861) — Lionel Stevenson

The Historic Churches of Prince Edward Island

Location and Index of Churches

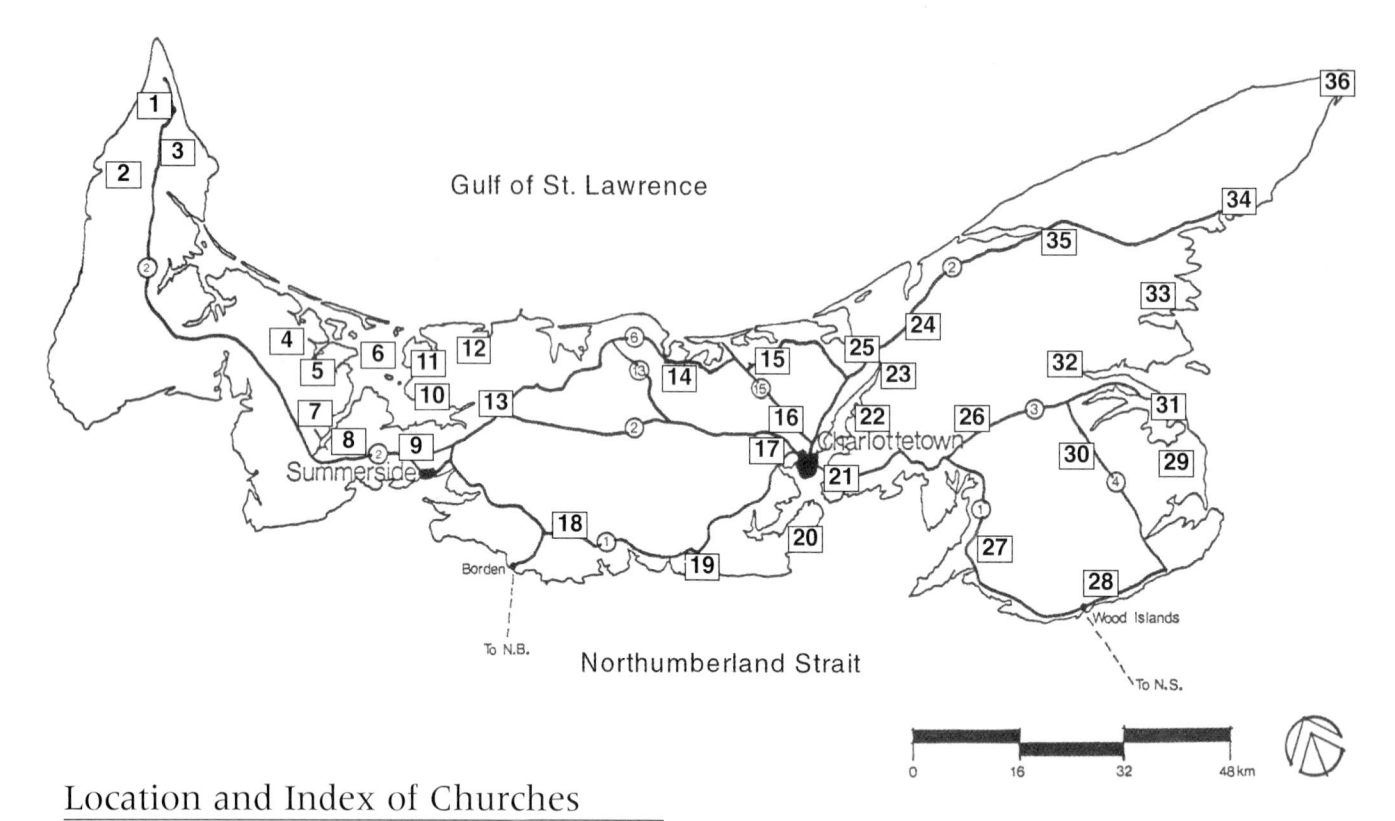

1. St. Simon and St. Jude Roman Catholic Church, *Tignish*, p. 67
2. Immaculate Conception Roman Catholic Church, *Palmer Road*, p. 110
3. Christ Church Anglican Church, *Kildare Capes*, p. 51
4. St. John's Anglican Church, *Ellerslie*, p. 80
5. St. James Anglican Church, *Port Hill*, p. 96
6. St. Ann's Roman Catholic Church, *Lennox Island*, p. 120
7. St. Patrick's Roman Catholic Church, *Grand River*, p. 55
8. St. John the Baptist Roman Catholic Church, *Miscouche*, p. 93
9. St. John's Anglican Church, *St. Eleanor's*, p. 102
10. St. Mary's Roman Catholic Church, *Indian River*, p. 59
11. Princetown United Church, *Malpeque*, p. 105
12. Geddie Memorial Church, *Springbrook*, p. 71
13. St. Mark's Anglican Church, *Kensington*, p. 108
14. St. Augustine's Roman Catholic Church, *South Rustico*, p. 82
15. St. James United Church, *West Covehead*, p. 98
16. South Winsloe United Church, *South Winsloe*, p. 54
17. St. John's Anglican Church, *Milton*, p. 101
18. Tryon United Church, p. 119
19. Free Church of Scotland, *Desable*, p. 78
20. St. Martin's Roman Catholic Church, *Cumberland*, p. 101
21. Cross Roads Christian Church, p. 104
22. Sacred Heart Roman Catholic Church, *Mount Ryan*, p. 56
23. St. Patrick's Roman Catholic Church, *Fort Augustine*, p. 91
24. St. Andrew's Chapel, p. 113
25. St. Bonaventure's Roman Catholic Church, *Tracadie Cross*, p. 84
26. St. Joachim's Roman Catholic Church, *Vernon River*, p. 115
27. St. John's Presbyterian Church, *Belfast*, p. 63
28. Little Sands United Church, *Little Sands*, p. 100
29. St Paul's Roman Catholic Church, *Sturgeon*, p. 87
30. Church of Christ, *Montague*, p. 57
31. Holy Trinity Anglican Church, *Georgetown*, p. 58
32. All Saints Roman Catholic Church, *Cardigan Bridge*, p. 94
33. St. Francis de Sales Roman Catholic Church, *Little Pond*, p. 120
34. St. Mary's Roman Catholic Church, *Souris*, p. 89
35. St. Peter's United Church, *St. Peter's Bay*, p. 118
36. East Point United Baptist Church, *East Point*, p. 107

In Charlottetown

37. All Souls' Chapel, St. Peter's Cathedral, p. 76
38. St. Paul's Anglican Church, p. 74
39. Central Christian Church, p. 25
40. St. Dunstan's Basilica, p. 53

In Summerside

41. St. Mary's Anglican Church, p. 24

Christ Church Anglican Church
Kildare Capes

This tiny church on the eastern shore of northern Prince County is typical of the many isolated rural churches in Prince Edward Island. Its clean, functional lines are enhanced by minimal ornamentation — elements of the neo-Gothic Style.

An Anglican church was begun on this site in 1851 but a missionary did not arrive until 1859, delaying the building's completion until 1861. Unfortunately, this church was burned to the ground in 1923, with only the organ being saved. A year later the Anglicans purchased a redundant Methodist church in Montrose and hauled it across the ice to the present site. After some alterations to the roofline and sanctuary the Anglicans had a fine replacement for the old church.

Christ Church stands on a small plot of land just off Route 12, and has a stunning view of the Gulf of St. Lawrence. Many sailors, whose ships floundered on the rocks below are buried in the cemetery.

Christ Church Anglican Church, Kildare Capes. – Lionel Stevenson

St. Dunstan's Basilica, Charlottetown. Extensive restorations, particularly of the two front towers, were begun in 1990 and are ongoing. St. Dunstan's was designated a National Historic Site in 1996.
　　　　　　　　　　　　– Lawrence McLagan

St. Dunstan's Basilica
Charlottetown

The soaring, two-hundred-foot spires of St. Dunstan's have been the most prominent landmark in Charlottetown since the Basilica was completed in 1919; this is the fourth Roman Catholic church to be built on the site since 1816. It replaced a similar stone cathedral, designed by a Quebec architect named Berlinguet, that burned to its foundations in 1913. The church was rebuilt in the Flamboyant Gothic Revival Style, in the form of a Gothic cross. Wallace, Nova Scotia sandstone and Miramichi freestone were used in the construction, and its design is undoubtedly architect John Hunter's finest achievement. A native of Scotland, Hunter moved to Charlottetown from Montreal after he received this commission.

Interior, St. Dunstan's Basilica, Charlottetown.
– Lawrence McLagan

The beautiful rose window, high on the west wall of the sanctuary of St. Dunstan's Basilica was crafted by F. Mayer in Munich, Germany, during the First World War. Its circular design represents eight of the patron saints and their attendant angels. The colour of the stained glass, even from the front of the church, is still vibrant and alive. *(see page 44)*

South Winsloe United Church, South Winsloe. – Scott Smith

South Winsloe United Church
South Winsloe

This tiny church in South Winsloe is one of the earliest brick churches in Prince Edward Island, and it is certainly the smallest. It was built in 1880 by Henry and Thomas Ford of Glasgow Road, replacing an earlier church built in 1850 by members of a Wesleyan Methodist sect called the Bible Christian Connexion. The land for the church was donated by one of Winsloe's early settlers, James Pickard. The bricks were fired at Rocky Point, and horse-and-sleigh convoys were sent through Charlottetown and across the winter ice to get them.

The building is very austere, with the only concession to decoration being the raised mouldings surrounding the heads of the Gothic door and windows. In 1960, the church was enlarged dramatically, when a vestry and full basement were added.

St. Patrick's Roman Catholic Church, Grand River. – Scott Smith

St. Patrick's Roman Catholic Church
Grand River

The present St. Patrick's Church was begun in 1836 and the interior completed in 1844. Distinctly English Gothic in style, it replaced two earlier churches: a small (32' x 18') log church with board-and-batten siding, built in 1810, and a larger, second church, built in 1818.

In 1890 this third church underwent an extensive renovation of its exterior, under the direction of Island architect William Harris.

He enlarged the original (60' x 40') plan, built a new steeple, redesigned the front entry and added Gothic clerestory windows. The result is quite successful, with the sham buttresses and clerestory giving the side elevations good composition and rhythm. Its characteristic ochre hue can be seen for miles across the lowlands of the Grand River, in Prince County.

Sacred Heart Roman Catholic Church
Johnston's River (Mount Ryan)

Sacred Heart Roman Catholic Church, Johnston's River (Mount Ryan).
— Scott Smith

    This unique church, designed by architects Chappel and Hunter, was built in 1916. Its Spanish Revival Style exhibits aspects of modernization — from the bellcast canopy over the front entry in the corner steeple to a Palladian-type window, with its centre section extended downward to form a cross. This window and a decorated parapet are the most prominent aspects of an interesting front gable.

    The church can be found at Johnston's River on Route 21, on the east side of the Hillsborough River, Queen's County.

Church of Christ
Montague

This church is one of the most elegantly proportioned buildings in Prince Edward Island. Its compact verticality and tall, round-headed windows are unmistakably Italianate and its commanding presence is a wonderful surprise to motorists entering Montague from the north on Main Street.

There is some documentation to suggest that architect John McLellan, a native of the Island and the designer of St. Joachim's Roman Catholic Church in nearby Vernon River, may have been involved in the design of this church as well. It was built at a cost of $6,000 and its walls of brick, made locally at Stewart's Brick Works, are still in excellent condition.

Church of Christ, Montague – Lionel Stevenson

The Church of Christ was built in 1876-79 by an association of independent Baptist congregations who had seceded from the Three Rivers Baptist Church some twenty years earlier. A new sanctuary and adjoining hall, sympathetically designed, was completed in 1989.

The first of three churches to be erected in the parish was built in 1814-1815 near the shore of Richmond Bay, on land donated by John and Angus MacLellan. It was a modest frame structure (40' x 36'), framed by Isaac Newton of Charlottetown and finished by members of the twenty-seven Roman Catholic families in the mission. It was later hauled inland to the site of the present church, but after the second church was completed in 1843, it appeared that the original structure was no longer needed. In 1853, however, the emerging town of Green's Shore, or Summerside, required a church building. The old church was dismantled in 1855 and hauled across the ice to its final resting place, where it remained in service until the late 1950s. This church no longer exists, but an old burying ground marks its original site.

In 1842 one of Reverend James MacDonald's first tasks was to build a parochial house and a new large church. In June of 1843, the cornerstone was laid and the church dedicated to The Blessed Virgin Mary. It was sometimes referred to as "Saint Mary's of the Pines." Built by Alexander MacLellan, it was an imposing frame structure for the time (90' x 50'), with fourteen-inch-square, hand-hewn hemlock timbers in the frame and a massive tower and spire that provided a magnificent view of the surrounding countryside. A parochial house was built at the same time in Grand River.

On August 4, 1896, as Reverend Monsignor D.J Gillis was saying his rosary on a nearby verandah, the church was struck by lightning and burned quickly to the ground. Monsignor Gillis and a Mr. Driscoll were able to save only the sacred vessels and a statue of the Virgin.

Statue of the Virgin, St. Mary's Roman Catholic Church, Indian River. – Lionel Stevenson

Although severely shaken by this unfortunate disaster, the redoubtable Monsignor Gillis soon began making plans for a new church.

"Yes, yes, build it like Kinkora, only bigger and better," Monsignor Gillis instructed architect William Harris. St. Malachy's at Kinkora had been built in 1899 and featured an impressive groined ceiling of lightly stained birch. Harris' design for St. Mary's is typical of his mature

Decorative trim, column capital, St. Mary's Roman Catholic Church, Indian River.
– Lionel Stevenson

Front facade, St. Mary's Roman Catholic Church, Indian River.
– Lionel Stevenson

French Gothic Style, based on models in Quebec, Britain and the United States. It too has a magnificent groined ceiling and nave arcades with a clerestory above them, but it is larger than St. Malachy's. Indeed, it is the largest wood church in Prince Edward Island. St. Mary's also differs in that its corner tower is round whereas St. Malachy's is square. Both churches possess principal elements of the French Gothic Style: a unified nave and chancel, apsidal sanctuary walls and shallow transepts. St. Malachy's differs in that it has an octagonal crossing. Both churches, but in particular St. Mary's, have excellent acoustics, a design priority in Harris' later career.

Construction began on St. Mary's in 1900 and was completed two years later at a cost of $20,000, much of which was donated by the parishioners and Monsignor Gillis himself. The new church, with a seating capacity of six hundred, was joined to a vestry which had served as a temporary chapel since the fire of 1896. The builder was Nathan MacFarlane and he was aided greatly in his task by a pervading spirit of civic cooperation — a spirit which prompted Thomas Tuplin and his sons to mill all the lumber for the church free of charge, and

John Walker of Kensington to donate all the lumber for the 128-foot spire. When completed in 1902, the church was entirely free of debt.

The exterior of the church is dominated by the cylindrical four-stage tower on the southwest corner. This tower contains the main entry and carries above it an octagonal spire with a band of arched niches at its base containing statues of the twelve apostles. Also noticeable are the bands of various shingle patterns that encircle not only the tower but the church proper. These shingles initially had an interesting colour scheme, as Harris intended, but today are painted white with black trim. The round tower enabled Harris to eliminate buttressing, and the reduction of buttresses around the rest of the building is a further indication of refinement in his mature style. Fenestration is predominantly hood-moulded lancets. A small lantern tops the roof crossing and the small flèches or spirelets decorate the transept eaves.

The focus of the interior is the east chancel with its neo-Gothic altar designed by William Harris himself. The exact location of this altar has varied. The cruciform plan, although common in Gothic churches, was most likely derived from French-Canadian models. On more than one occasion, Harris had visited Montreal to inspect churches of a similar style. He also designed a pulpit that could be lowered with a system of pulleys and weights into the basement, but this was never built. A repetitive motif in the interior is the hexagon, seen in the ceiling and floor of the west tower entry and in the six-leafed rosette windows in the transept walls and the west wall. *(see page 38)* The interior wood finishes, from the varnished white pine of the

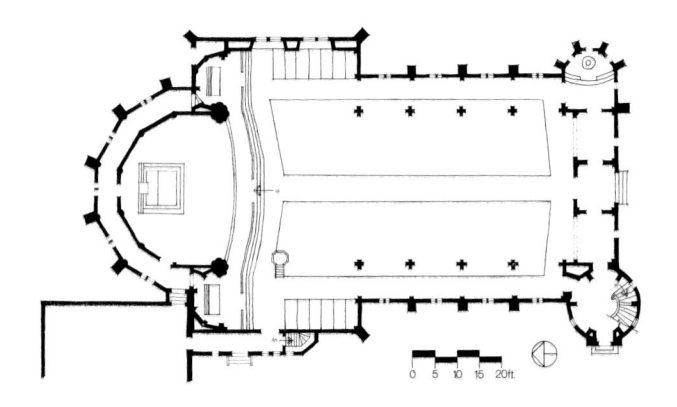

FLOOR PLAN: *St. Mary's Roman Catholic Church, Indian River.*

church furniture to the darker cherry wood of the ceiling ribs, mouldings and clustered column shafts with carved capitals, generate considerable warmth. St. Mary's offers further evidence of Harris' later preoccupation with acoustical perfection. The acoustics are superb — at least when the church is empty. There are five organs in the church, but the main organ is located in the choir loft at the west end of the nave.

The architectural highlights of St. Mary's are numerous. It is unfortunate that the main church is used for only two months of the year. Services are held for the small congregation in the vestry for the remainder of the year. The building was unheated for 35 years and deterioration, particularly of the plastered walls and shingling, was extensive. The Friends of St. Mary's, organized in 1986, were able to save the church from destruction through an intense fund-raising effort. In 1996 the first summer music festival was held within its walls. The Indian River Festival has since become an extremely popular summer event. (see also front cover, pages 35, 38, 42, 47)

St. John's Presbyterian Church
Belfast (Pinette)

One of the most charming and historic of all Island churches is St. John's Presbyterian Church in Belfast, King's County. It was begun in 1824 and completed in 1826 by Selkirk settlers who had immigrated to the Island from the Scottish Highlands some twenty years earlier. They were directed in their task by the designer of the church, Robert Jones, a highly skilled and well-respected cabinet-maker born near Paisley, Scotland, in 1779. Jones emigrated in 1809. On his arrival in Prince Edward Island, he worked as a shipjoiner and lumber surveyor. In 1815 he was operating Lord Selkirk's lumber mill on the Pinette River, near Belfast. In 1824 Jones responded to an advertisement in the Prince Edward Island *Register* and was awarded the contract to build a new church at Pinette. The new church replaced the original log structure built in 1804 by John Gillis, a native of the Isle of Skye. The first services in the log church were conducted by the settlement's physician, Dr. Angus MacAuley, who was also an ordained Church of Scotland minister. The first full-time minister was Reverend John MacLennan, who arrived from Scotland in 1823.

St. John's Presbyterian Church, Belfast. – Lionel Stevenson

Interior views, St. John's Presbyterian Church, Belfast. — Lionel Stevenson

Robert Jones was a meticulous builder who kept a diary of the daily activities, and his efficient and precise building habits pleased the Reverend MacLennan immensely. The lumber for the church was milled at Lord Selkirk's mill and hauled just up the hill to where the church was being built in a grove of maple trees. The hardwood shingles, which remain to this day, were hand-split with a mallet and a primitive wedge-like instrument called a "frow", (or froe) then fastened to the exterior of the church with iron nails hand-forged by the local blacksmith.

Although the exterior of St. John's shows remarkable fidelity to its original design, the interior has undergone numerous changes. In 1864 the church was reshingled and the inside walls were plastered. A vestry was also added behind the choir, at the east end of the church. Around the turn of the century the original box pews, each with its own entry gate, were removed in favour of more contemporary ones, and the old high pulpit was replaced by the present one, built on a raised platform. In 1922 the building was raised twenty-two inches and the original stone foundation was replaced with one of concrete. Four years later, the four original wood-burning stoves were replaced with two furnaces, the vestry was extended and the entire building was repainted. Another major renovation took place in 1938, during which the walls and ceiling were refinished with diagonal tongue-and-groove cladding, and four memorial windows were installed in the east wall behind the pulpit. (A fifth was added later.) This renovation proved so extensive that the church was consequently rededicated.

Hand grained woodwork and pews, St. John's Presbyterian Church, Belfast.
— Lionel Stevenson

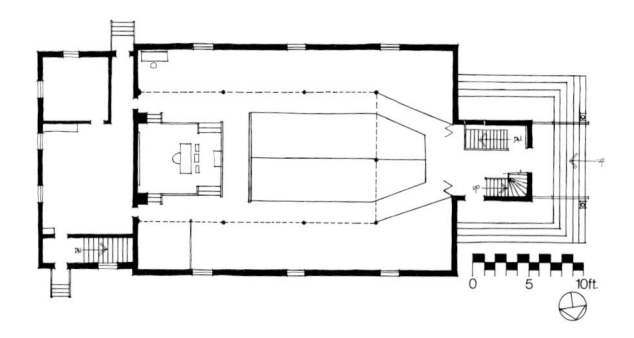

FLOOR PLAN: *St. John's Presbyterian Church, Belfast.*

The style of the church is basic neo-Classic meeting house architecture with superimposed elements of the Gothic Revival. The four-stage tower is a derivative of the elemental designs of Sir Christopher Wren, most notably the tower of St. Dunstan's in the East, in London, England. Robert Jones was undoubtedly influenced by Wren's churches during his earlier apprenticeship in London. The slender spire atop the tower, eighty-five feet tall at its apex, was added later, in 1860, and built by Neil and Malcolm MacLeod of Orwell. The present church bell is inscribed "St. John's Church 1834," but there is evidence that an earlier bell was cracked in a collapse of the bell tower and sent to England to be recast.

St. John's, the earliest extant Presbyterian place of worship erected on the Island, is a building of simple, dignified charm. The nave windows, with their Gothic tracery and labels; the beautifully proportioned, tiered bell tower and spire, sixteen by fourteen feet at its base; and the delightful, four-panel entry doors are a tribute to Robert Jones' integrity and skill as a designer and builder. The well-maintained interior is highlighted by its compact floor plan and the five memorial windows on the east wall. A gallery that encircles the north, south and west walls is supported by hand-grained wood columns.

The first services conducted in the church

Four tiered tower and spire, St. John's Presbyterian Church, Belfast. – Lionel Stevenson

Tower entry and window, St. John's Presbyterian Church, Belfast. Window: pointed gothic with perpendicular tracery. – Lionel Stevenson

were in Gaelic, but an expanding English-speaking congregation led to the later construction of the "tent," a large frame structure built beside the church to accommodate nearly two thousand people. Prior to its erection, communion services were held outdoors, and until 1910 English-speaking and Gaelic parishioners held separate services. There is some evidence of small windows in the east and west walls of the church where the minister and bell-ringer, respectively, could administer to and observe these peripheral services. The church has alternately been called "Pinette Church" or "Belfast Church" but the parish has always been the parish of St. John, named by Captain Samuel Holland in 1764.

(see also pages 32, 40)

St. Simon and St. Jude Roman Catholic Church
Tignish

St. Simon and St. Jude Roman Catholic Church is the focal point and civic heart of the historic Acadian-Irish town of Tignish. Its spire dominates the surrounding landscape and for decades has been a welcome beacon for local fishermen.

The original Tignish was founded on a nearby shore in 1799 by eight Acadian families who had immigrated there from Malpeque in open boats. They built the first church in Tignish in 1801, a simple log building (30' x 25'). It stood at the northeast corner of the old cemetery, the last remaining evidence of this early settlement. In 1811 two Irishmen, Edward and Michael Reilly, came to the area by boat from Richibucto, New Brunswick and landed in the Nail Pond area. They established the first Irish community in the immediate vicinity. In 1826 the second church was built, a two-storey, neo-Classic building (60' x 45'). It was built under the supervision of William Harper, a master carpenter brought over from Percé, Quebec. When the present church was built in 1860, this second church was hauled to a more central location, renamed St. Mary's Hall and used regularly as a grammar school and parish hall until 1964 when it collapsed during a second attempt to relocate it.

St. Simon and St. Jude Roman Catholic Church, Tignish.
– Scott Smith

In 1857 through the influence of Reverend Sylvain-Ephrem Poirier, Father Peter MacIntyre hired an architect from New York named P.C. Keely, along with his assistant, Owen Hamill, to design and supervise construction of a new church for Tignish. The assembly of local materials, including a half-million bricks made at Francis Hughes' brickyard just outside the town, had begun three full years earlier.

The brick manufacturing process was described in the 1960 Church Centennial souvenir program thus:

"The method used was primitive, but the results lasting. The clay was dug and placed in what was called a pug-mill. This contained staves and blades. The power used was furnished by a horse going round and round to rotate the blades. The mass of the clay was then taken out, mixed with shore sand and kneaded like bread, placed in wooden moulds, wheeled to a "hake," where the wind swept through the layers of brick, partly drying them. A kiln was built, lined with brick and covered with sod. Huge sticks of hardwood were burned to bake the brick."

Except for the freestone buttress tops and roof slates, both now removed, the church was built entirely of materials found within the parish. An ardent student of A.W. Pugin, architect Keely designed and built several other churches in this High Gothic Style, including a similar building in Bangor, Maine. However St. Simon and St. Jude may well have been his most austere and refined Gothic statement, its design showing affinities to Pugin's St. Oswald's in Liverpool, England (no longer extant). This church is a magnificent statement indeed. Its 165-foot steeple soars above the town, and the

Mural by François-Xavier Édouard Meloche. St. Simon and St. Jude Roman Catholic Church, Tignish. – Ken MacKinnon

exhilaration at its completion prompted one of the young workers, Joseph Bernard, to perform a headstand on the very top of the steeple. Stones for the foundation were brought by boat and horse-drawn carts from Lot 7, and interior columns and decorative woodwork were cut from pine trees found on the Centre Line Road. Gravel and lime were brought to Tignish from

A station of the cross, St. Simon and St. Jude Roman Catholic Church, Tignish. — Scott Smith

Arched doorway, St. Simon and St. Jude Roman Roman Catholic Church, Tignish. — Lionel Stevenson

Miminegash and sand was found on local shores. The building of the church took fourteen months, and so efficient was Father MacIntyre's management that any debts incurred by the parish were erased within one year of the Church's completion.

Father MacIntyre was called to become the third Bishop of Charlottetown before the work was completed, but on August 19, 1860, he brought a host of clergymen with him to Tignish for the consecration of the new church. Such a grand public assembly has not been seen since in Tignish. The overflowing crowd unanimously endorsed the church's design, with its soaring, buttressed tower, delicate side-aisle entries and small Lady Chapel extending north from the west side of the Sanctuary. MacLellan Brothers of Summerside did the initial interior work and, although the decoration was not completed until 1885, there was much to admire. François-Xavier Édouard Meloche, a prominent painter/architect from Montreal was hired to redecorate what was felt to be a dark and ponderous interior. With the help of twelve apprentices he brightened the church considerably and developed a coherent iconographic cycle for the perimeter walls. Ten of the apostles were painted in sepia or "grisaille" and St. Simon and St. Jude were rendered in colour to give them special emphasis. As well, large colour paintings of the Transfiguration and the Assumption of the Virgin were painted on either side of the sanctuary and a false clerestory effect was achieved above the nave arcades.

Other highlights of the interior include William Profit's decorative woodcarving and the earliest complete stained glass cycle on the Island. Meloche's decorative paintings and the stained glass blend well to give the interior a pleasing consistency.

A magnificent tracker action pipe organ, one of the finest in the Maritimes, was built for the church by Louis Mitchell of Montreal and installed in 1882. In 1886 the larger of the two bells was blessed and installed in the steeple. A convent was built in 1868 and a parochial house in 1872, both of Hughes' brick. An extensive redecoration took place from 1950 to 1952. The ornate Gothic altar, once removed, has recently been replaced, but Meloche's paintings, done in a High Renaissance style, survive in their original state. In July 1960 the one-hundredth Anniversary of the church was celebrated. St. Simon and St. Jude Roman Catholic Church, now the spiritual centre for seven hundred families, is a fitting architectural symbol of civic co-operation of which the citizens of Tignish can be justly proud.

Interior, St. Simon and St. Jude Roman Catholic Church, Tignish. Tracker organ by Louis Mitchell of Montreal. – Lionel Stevenson

Bell tower and Geddie Memorial Church, Springbrook.
– Lionel Stevenson

Geddie Memorial Church
Springbrook

In Springbrook, on a hill overlooking the placid waters of New London harbour on Prince Edward Island's north shore, stands the Geddie Memorial Church, one of the Island's most historic and well-preserved churches. The church was built in 1836-1837 by James Clark, using timber cut from the forest by members of the congregation. Lime for the wall plaster was provided by women who burned oyster shells gathered from nearby shores. The deed for the church land and cemetery was bought from Alexander Anderson in 1842 for the sum of three British pounds. For twenty-eight years thereafter, the church was still referred to as "Anderson's church."

Reverend Dr. John Geddie, a native of Banff, Scotland, was ordained and inducted in the pastoral charge of Cavendish and New London North in March of 1838. A survivor of a serious childhood illness and a man of small physical stature and frail constitution, Geddie devoted his life to God's service at an early age. He spread the Presbyterian word throughout the Island with great energy, enduring many hardships in his travels across the parish with his horse, Sampson. Although dedicated to his home mission, Geddie felt a call to minister in foreign fields. In 1844 he submitted an overture before the Synod of the Presbyterian Church of Nova Scotia for the support of a foreign mission. In 1845 it was approved and Geddie subsequently resigned from his charge and volunteered for a mission on the primitive South Pacific island of Aneiteum in the New Hebrides. He thus became the first Canadian Presbyterian foreign missionary, and his efforts are summarized on a tablet hanging on the west wall of the church. It reads in part, "When he landed there were no Christians and when he left, there were no heathens." Geddie returned to Prince Edward Island briefly in 1864, but in 1871 he went to Australia for health reasons. He worked on Old Testament translations until his death there in December 1872.

The church at Springbrook is a fitting memorial to this remarkable man. It replaced an earlier log church built by Reverend Dr. Keir in 1810 at Yankee Hill. The old pewter communion service that now sits in a cabinet below the pulpit was

Reverend Dr. John Geddie.

taken from this old church. Many other artifacts and relics of Reverend Dr. Geddie's missionary experience were donated to the church by the Fraser family.

Among them are a sample of cloth from the South Sea Islands, a picture of Mrs. Geddie and three members of her family, and a three-foot-long New Hebridian war club. On the west wall hangs a framed copy of Geddie's farewell address and behind the pulpit stand two chairs that had been used in the Geddie home. The church was lit for many years by two cabin lights salvaged from the clipper *Marco Polo*, which went down off the New London shore. A visitors' register, with Florentine-tooled leather binding, was presented to the church in 1917 by the Island's gifted author, Lucy Maud Montgomery.

The clean, simple lines of the church (with its unique twelve-over-eight window sashes) have remained unchanged over the years, but in 1904 some alterations were made to the interior. The square box pews were replaced with new ones and the high pulpit was lowered and rebuilt with wood from the old pews. The walls were completely redecorated at this time as well. In 1905 the late H.C. MacLeod donated an eight hundred pound bell to the church; the structure, however, was inadequate to carry the weight. A separate bell tower, designed by Major Schurman and built by John Warren, was constructed through the fund-raising efforts of Mrs. Lucy Ferguson. On July 1, 1905, the bell was first rung by George Ferguson, who continued in this role for another fifty years or more. The church received electricity in 1956, and recently a new concrete block foundation was built. In 1984, the exterior of the church was repainted and the interior completely redecorated in a colour scheme of ochre and brown that is most appropriate.

The congregation elected to remain Presbyterian at Church Union in 1925. The church continues to serve a small but dedicated congregation that should be commended for its efforts in preserving this unique old church and its beautiful grounds, cemetery and stone war memorial. The interior, with its raised pulpit and gallery around three sides, is a model of austere and unpretentious design. The furnishings and mementos of Reverend Dr. Geddie's career give the church a characteristic warmth.
(see also pages 37, 46)

Interior, Geddie Memorial Church, Springbrook
– Lionel Stevenson

St. Paul's Anglican Church
Charlottetown

The parish of Charlotte in Charlottetown was the first Anglican parish in Prince Edward Island, established in 1769. It was also the first parish to have an appointed rector — the Reverend Theophilus Desbrisay — in 1774. The first church was built in 1800, near the site of the present one. The second church, built in 1836, was replaced by William Harris' masterpiece in 1896. A triumph in Island sandstone, St. Paul's is probably Harris' most unified and complete Island church in the French Gothic Revival Style. The church, rectory (1889) and hall (1906), all in sandstone, form an important architectural complex at the east end of Queen Square.

The interior of the church is one of the most thoroughly calculated and aesthetically pleasing of Harris' churches. An article in the *Charlot-*

St. Paul's Anglican Church, Charlottetown. — Lawrence McLagan

tetown Examiner of March 14, 1896, best describes the acoustical quality of the church:

"The wooden groined roof covering the chancel and nave, besides being beautiful, is acoustically a very valuable feature, as abrupt square surfaces at right angles throughout the building are thus avoided and the resonant qualities of the smooth spruce boards are very valuable. The octagonal shape of the end of the

St. Paul's Anglican Church, Charlottetown. – drawing by R.C. Tuck

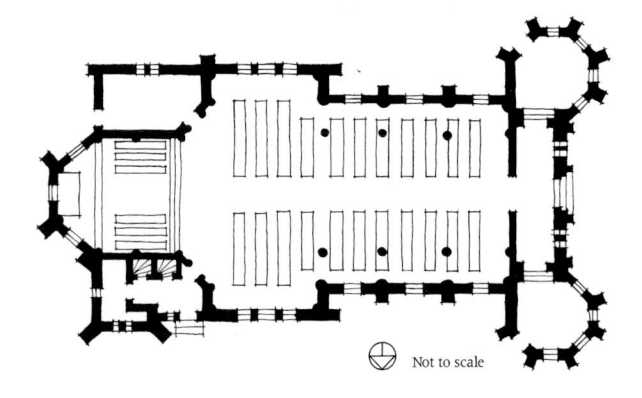

FLOOR PLAN: *St. Paul's Anglican Church, Charlottetown.*

sanctuary, with its roof curving outwards towards the nave, has the effect of reflecting the millions of sound waves from the singing and organ pipes directly into the body of the church, thus intensifying a hundredfold in tone all the sound that is produced."

Harris was an enthusiastic amateur musician, and he designed this church interior with as much attention to acoustics as if he were designing a violin. He built resonating panels of maple and spruce into the chancel walls that, together with the darkly stained, groined ceilings, provide excellent sound projection into the nave. However, on occasion, speakers and musicians have experienced some difficulty in hearing themselves.

The remainder of the interior finish woodwork, done by H. and S. Lowe and the Whitlock brothers, creates an atmosphere of great richness and warmth. The exquisite wood panelling, the beautifully carved column capitals and arches, the embossed ceramic tiles on the chancel walls, made at the Prince Edward Island Pottery, and the parquet floor in the sanctuary are all artistically executed details that contribute to the overall harmony of the interior. The oak pulpit and communion table are also highly ornate and built to Harris' designs. The rolled "cathedral" glass windows, particularly in the south transept wall, are quite distinctive. The rose window in this wall was imported from England in 1873 and transferred from the old church. The lack of a clerestory is an asset. The reduced light creates a subdued ambiance that is, to this observer, most attractive.

An interesting feature of this church, added in 1979, is the semicircular pedestrian ramp at the west entry. Regardless of its aesthetic merit, it is an early example of an attempt by a church to accommodate its handicapped parishioners.

The twin octagonal vestries that flank the main entry were built in 1920 as memorials to those who served in the First World War.
(see also page 38)

All Souls' Chapel, St. Peter's Cathedral, Charlottetown.
– Lawrence McLagan

All Souls' Chapel
Charlottetown

Originally called the Hodgson Memorial Chapel in memory of Reverend George Hodgson, who died in 1885, All Souls' Chapel represents, in the opinion of many, architect William Harris' finest career achievement. The chapel is a beautifully proportioned addition to the west wall of St. Peter's Cathedral on Rochford Street in Charlottetown, and was built entirely of rust-red Island sandstone in the High Victorian, Gothic Revival Style. Lowe Brothers of Charlottetown were the contractors, and the Chapel, begun in 1888, took six years to complete. The interior is

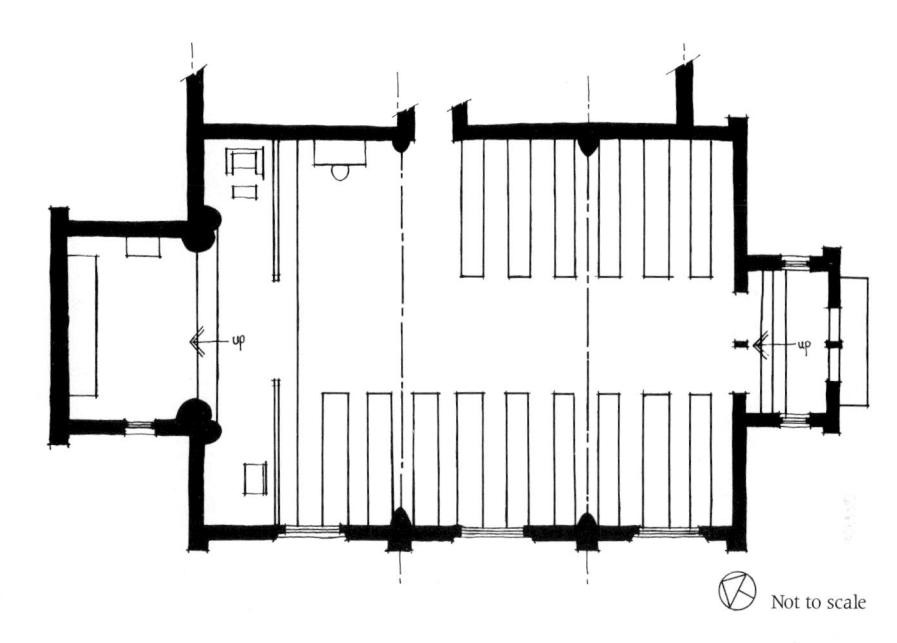

FLOOR PLAN: *All Souls' Chapel, St. Peter's Cathedral, Charlottetown.*

Not to scale

highly ornate and evokes a sense of mystery *(see p. 45)*. The subdued lighting, the walnut altar and reredos, the dark oak and walnut panelling by woodcarvers Whitlock and Doull, and a delicately carved stone arch fronting the sanctuary give the interior a richness and warmth of profound magnitude. Eighteen paintings by Robert Harris, the architect's brother, give distinction to the interior, and his *Ascension of Christ* (1898) in the sanctuary provides a focal point. All Souls' Chapel was built almost entirely by Island craftsmen, but an outstanding contribution is the stained glass of the chapel's windows by Kempe and Sons of London, England. The Chapel is full of memorials to prominent clergymen and other civic leaders. Memorial tablets, paintings and pieces of church furniture surround the interior, but there is still ample evidence of the skills and dedication of Robert Harris and his brother William. A "memorial" interior can be difficult for a designer to control; however, the brothers Harris have, in this case, done so with taste and reverence.

Reverend F.E.J. Lloyd, curate of the Cathedral, claimed in the *Charlottetown Examiner* that the chapel, "for design, construction, beauty and general arrangement surpasses anything yet seen in Canada in connection with the Anglican Church...."

In 1994, All Souls' was designated a National Historic Site. (see also pages 42, 45)

Free Church of Scotland
Desable

The Free Church of Scotland at Desable is distinctive among Island churches, mostly because of its internal planning. It was one of the first churches erected for Reverend Donald McDonald, a missionary of the Church of Scotland, who established a local sect called the "McDonaldites" in the mid-1800s.

Reverend Donald McDonald was a controversial figure within the Church of Scotland (he never formally joined the Kirk Presbytery of the Maritimes), and the value of his writings will long be debated. Nonetheless, he was a missionary of great energy and dedication to his many widespread congregations. During his more than forty years of ministry, through zealous labours he managed to convert thousands to his faith during two major periods of revival. "The Minister" was a man of great charisma, and his services, often performed free of charge, would usually begin with a resume of the leading events of the day. His sermons, sometimes in English and sometimes in Gaelic, were powerful and thoroughly Calvinistic. Hymn singing was done in the old style of chanting one line at a time. His services were also known for "the works," a series of bodily movements throughout the congregation. These were spasmodic physical reactions which expressed the congregation's religious fervour.

Reverend Donald McDonald came to Prince Edward Island in 1826 and, travelling on footpaths, spread the gospel from house to house across a parish ninety miles long. At the time of his death, in 1867, his followers numbered five thousand. He had built fourteen churches, most of which were oriented on their transverse axis, with the raised pulpit on the north side of the nave. Directly in front of the pulpit, the elders sat on an elevated platform surrounded by a railing. One of these elders, called the precentor

Free Church of Scotland, Desable. – Lionel Stevenson

Gabled niches on spire of Free Church of Scotland, Desable.
—Lionel Stevenson

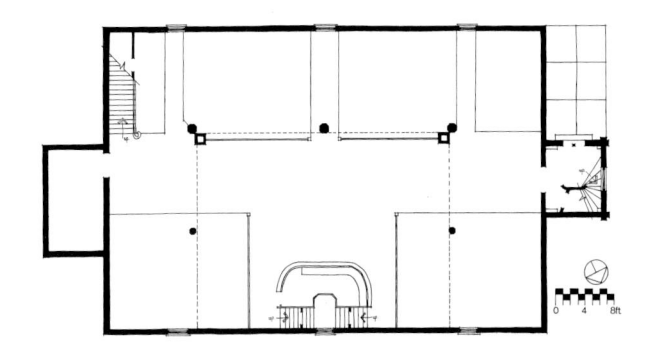

FLOOR PLAN: *Free Church of Scotland, Desable.*

(or preceptor), usually led the singing of the psalms in Gaelic. This church, including the upper gallery, will accommodate five hundred people, although there are accounts of twice that number attending some of McDonald's services. The seating is arranged in both north-south and east-west directions, and for a long time men and women were seated in different sections. This is meeting house architecture and is essentially derived from New England models of a slightly earlier period.

The present church is the second one on the site, and what a beautiful site it is! Situated on a wooded hill overlooking the Desable River, it commands a magnificent view of the surrounding countryside and is a landmark for travellers by land or sea.

Since its erection in 1855, the church has undergone little physical change. The original square tower was improved by the addition of an octagonal spire with a delightful wrought iron thistle at its peak. The Scottish thistle motif prevails throughout the church, from the graphic woodwork on the tower to the delicate hand-carving by Mr. J. Weeks on the pulpit and gallery face. In 1931 the old pews were replaced with new ones; and in 1946 the original red pine shingles and a secondary layer of cedar shingles were removed (with some difficulty) and the roof was reshingled. In 1980 a new concrete step was installed at the front door. Apart from periodic repairs and redecorating, the church has retained its simple, graceful lines and understated charm. Its interior, though devoid of much ornamentation, is quite warm, due to an abundance of richly grained wood surfaces.

Reverend Donald McDonald was a colourful and dedicated evangelist, and reminders of his unique brand of religion are still very much alive on the Island, in churches like this one at Desable. After his death in 1867, McDonald's congregations elected to join the Free Church of Scotland, which had seceded from the Church of Scotland in 1843. *(see also pages 19, 46)*

St. John's Anglican Church, Ellerslie. – Lionel Stevenson

St. John's Anglican Church
Ellerslie

St. John's Anglican Church in Ellerslie is indeed a gem of a church, representing perhaps Harry Williams' finest hour as a craftsman, although the frame for the building was erected by Edward England. The church was begun in 1894, but was not completed until 1899 and consecrated in 1900. Later, structural problems of lateral stability developed and it became necessary to install iron tie rods to reinforce the roof trusses.

England, who also donated the land for the church, did some of the interior woodcarving, but the bulk of the finish work was left for "Little" Harry Williams. A native of Poplar Grove

Front facade, St. John's Anglican Church, Ellerslie.
– Lionel Stevenson

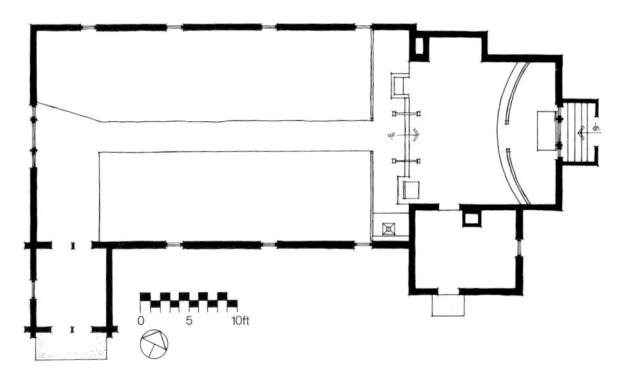

FLOOR PLAN: *St. John's Anglican Church, Ellerslie.*

and a descendant of some of the Island's most prominent master carpenters and shipbuilders, Williams studied architectural design in Massachusetts. A meticulous craftsman, he fabricated most of the interior ornamental work and the door and window frames and sashes in his home workshop. His desire for perfection and quality can be seen both inside and outside this beautiful church. The complex shingle patterns on the facades and steeple are ingeniously executed, and the decorated freize below the eaves and the ornate window hood moulds give the facades a depth of character that is not often found in small rural churches. Wherever one looks at this church, interesting detail is found; the flag motif below the front nave window and the delicate finial at the roof's crest are two such examples.

The interior is no different. Harry Williams and Edward England have obviously referred to their shipbuilding ancestry in the framing of the roof. The ceiling panels are arranged in exquisite rectilinear patterns, and the richly stained framing members and decorative trim give the interior warmth. The stained glass windows in the sanctuary add colour to this exhilarating interior.

"Little" Harry Williams has captured the inspirational essence of church architecture and has perfectly matched it to the scale of this building. The art of the builder is itself an inspiration; no aspect of the building seems superfluous. The aesthetic balance within and without this church is a rare and outstanding achievement.

(see also pages 6, 39)

St. Augustine's Roman Catholic Church
South Rustico

St. Augustine's Roman Catholic Church in the historic village of South Rustico is a model of ornamentation with restraint in church architecture. Its multi-paned, paired Gothic windows and quatrefoil motif in the tower's woodwork give this church a grandeur that is achieved through well-calculated, detailed design, rather than size and extravagance.

Although the church was completed in the autumn of 1838, it was not until the summer of 1845 that the interior was finally lathed and plastered. The church was built by local Acadian carpenters under the supervision of Bishop Bernard Donald MacDonald, who continued to reside in South Rustico even though the Diocesan headquarters were in Charlottetown. St. Augustine's served as a pro-cathedral until a suitable building could be constructed in Charlottetown.

St. Augustine's Roman Catholic Church, South Rustico.
– Lionel Stevenson

St. Augustine's Roman Catholic Church, South Rustico. — Lionel Stevenson

The present church replaces two earlier churches in the community, a log church that was built near the old cemetery in 1795 and a larger church built on the present site in 1806-1807. The three bells in the church tower were purchased in London, England, during the ministry (1859-1869) of Father George-Antoine Belcourt, an energetic and distinguished clergyman and founder of South Rustico's historic Farmers' Bank (1864). The tower had to be reinforced in the early 1900s; and the stone archway at the front entrance, with its commemorative plaques listing the successive priests at the church, was built in 1938.

St. Augustine's dramatic and contrasting appearance make it a landmark in this charming village on Prince Edward Island's north shore, Queen's County. *(see also page 12)*

St. Bonaventure's Roman Catholic Church
Tracadie Cross

St. Bonaventure's Roman Catholic Church, Tracadie Cross.
— Lionel Stevenson

The MacDonald settlers, under the supervision and protection of Captain John MacDonald of Glenaladale, Scotland, arrived on Prince Edward Island — then St. John's Island — between 1772 and 1775. Hundreds of immigrants from South Uist and other parts of Invernesshire, in the Scottish Highlands, settled in the Tracadie Bay and Scotchfort areas of Lots 35 and 36, of which Captain MacDonald was proprietor. This area had earlier been settled by Acadians. After the Expulsion of 1758, one of the few buildings remaining from their community, the old wooden chapel at Scotchfort, was found partially in ruins. Although it was quite small (30' x 25') with ten-foot ceilings, it was restored under the direction of Father James

Interior, St. Bonaventure's Roman Catholic Church, Tracadie Cross. — Lionel Stevenson

MacDonald. It served this growing community of Scottish pioneers well, until just prior to 1840, when Reverend James Brady built the first church on the present site. This church was much larger (60' x 40'). In 1864 a tower was built and other additions were made under the direction of Reverend Thomas Phelan.

The present St. Bonaventure's Roman Catholic Church was built in 1903, twenty-five yards from the earlier church, which has since been destroyed. It was designed in neo-Gothic style by a Quebec architect, R.P. Lemay, and was built by Francis Bradley of Kelly's Cross and Patrick and James Bradley of St. Theresa's, under the supervision of Reverends P.J. Hogan and P.E. McGuigan. These carpenters showed great skill, particularly in the construction of the groined ceilings of alternating horizontal and diagonal tongue-and-groove birch cells, trimmed with oak and walnut mouldings. The detail and craftsmanship of the oak communion and sanctuary rails and the sanctuary wainscoting are also impressive. The carved mouldings and rosettes around the Gothic windows and the pine column capitals give the interior warmth and texture. The length of the church, from the back of the semi-circular sanctuary to the front vestibule, is 105 feet, and the width of the nave is fifty-three feet. The side chapel (20' x 18') and the church can seat approximately 650 people altogether.

St. Bonaventure's is decidedly French Gothic Revival in style. Its assymetrically located tower, sham buttresses, groin vaulting, semi-circular apse and Gothic windows are all major elements of the French Gothic Revival Style. The tower, fourteen feet square, rises 112 feet to the top of the cross. The buttressed campanile or bell tower, with its four corner pinnacles, stands twenty-three feet above the main ridge. The door and window hood mouldings, clapboard siding, corner boards and buttresses, clerestory and spire give the church a well-calculated balance between the vertical and the horizontal.

The church is a pleasant surprise to anyone driving in the Tracadie Cross area. It is located at the intersection of Routes 218 and 219, not far from the southernmost tip of Tracadie Bay.
(see also page 36)

Tower entry, St. Bonaventure's Roman Catholic Church, Tracadie Cross.
– Lionel Stevenson

St. Paul's Roman Catholic Church, Sturgeon. – Lionel Stevenson

St. Paul's Roman Catholic Church
Sturgeon

St. Paul's Roman Catholic Church in Sturgeon was built in 1888. Constructed primarily of Island sandstone, the string courses and window and door arches are of Nova Scotia freestone, which was brought to Prince Edward Island by boat.

With guidance from Reverend William Phelan, an Irishman from County Wexford now buried in the vault beneath the altar, the building was designed by architect William Harris. St. Paul's was Harris' first Roman Catholic Church, as well as his first stone church, and although it exhibits the monumentality of the Romanesque Revival spirit, its design is essentially French Gothic.

The influence of New Brunswick designer and builder Reverend Edward Medley, a major proponent of Gothic Revival church architecture, is evident in this church. The windowless aisle walls and the narrow lancet windows grouped in threes in the clerestory above were Medley-inspired techniques to effect light falling from above. It appears as if the nave was built too high and narrow to achieve this effect. With the subsequent addition of side-aisle dormers, one must wonder about the success of the original design.

The stone for the church was quarried on nearby St. Mary's Road. It is interesting to note that the size of the blocks diminishes with the height of the walls. This contributes to the verticality of the building, along with the high nave, lancet windows, and asymmetrically placed steeple with broach spire.

The interior was not finished until 1892 when the church was dedicated. In 1973 it underwent a drastic modernization: the interior was completely repainted, new pews were installed, and due to a liturgical change, the original high altar with reredos was replaced with a plain communion table. The effects of this modernization are to be questioned, as the interior seems to have lost some of its focus and warmth. Moreover, it has betrayed the period character of the building. There is an unfortunate tension between the warmth and fidelity of the exterior and the superimposed contemporary design of the interior. *(see also page 45)*

Pointed lancet window detail, St. Paul's Roman Catholic Church, Sturgeon.
— Lionel Stevenson

St. Mary's Roman Catholic Church, Souris. — Lionel Stevenson

St. Mary's Roman Catholic Church, Souris, before the disastrous fire of 1928.
— Public Archives of Prince Edward Island

St. Mary's Roman Catholic Church
Souris

St. Mary's Roman Catholic Church in Souris is a massive structure built of sandstone. The church has a tragic history of fires. The first church (60' x 35') was founded by Reverend John MacDonald of Glenaladale in 1839, but ten years later, it and a fine parochial house were destroyed by fire. A second church was opened in November 1849, and a new parochial house was built by Revereend James Phelan in 1862. This second church was subsequently demolished in 1901, and the present church was built to a design of William Harris. It is one of the largest in Prince Edward Island (194' x 80'), with seating for twelve hundred people. The construction of the church was undertaken by MacEachern and Duffy of Souris, with the exterior completed in 1902 and the interior a year later. It was built almost entirely of Island sandstone, quarried at nearby Chepstow; however Nova Scotia freestone was used in the string courses and window and door arches. The use of the round and truncated towers were innovations in Harris' design style, as was the use of decorative rings of lighter-coloured bricks in the tower's cornice detail. The original spire, 150 feet tall, was built by Mr. Duffy, and the roof construction, a sophisticated system of framing in those days, was supervised by Bernard Creamer of Souris.

In 1928 disaster struck again and the church was entirely gutted by a fire caused by a defective flue. Reconstruction began almost immediately and, in 1930, the church was re-opened. Architect John Hunter was quite sympathetic to Harris' original design, although the interior is less Gothic in its detailing than that of its predecessor. All the stone walls were retained, but some had to be rebuilt to a slightly different design and a clerestory was added. The tall spire was destroyed in the blaze and was replaced with a more ornate, octagonal, neo-Baroque brick cap that is not consistent with the overall style of the building. In the late 1950s, the interior of the church was extensively redecorated under the direction of Monsignor Murphy. In 1975 the slate shingles were removed from the roof and replaced by heavy asphalt shingles. A new pipe organ was recently installed as well.

St. Mary's Roman Catholic Church is located at the crest of a rise of land in west central Souris, with a magnificent view of the Souris River and Colville Bay.

Gallery stair and cabinet, St. Mary's Roman Catholic Church, Souris. – Lionel Stevenson

St. Patrick's Roman Catholic Church, Fort Augustus.
– Lionel Stevenson

St. Patrick's Roman Catholic Church
Fort Augustus

St. Patrick's Roman Catholic Church has been called "the truest Gothic church on the Island," and it is easy to see why. Its buttressed nave and central steeple, Gothic windows and high, rib-vaulted ceiling make it one of the most well-defined examples of the Gothic Revival idiom. It is also one of architect William Harris' most impressive interiors. The vaulting, which extends the entire 131-foot length of the church, is painted a light colour. Dark brown accents on

Arched doorway and statue, St. Patrick's Roman Catholic Church, Fort Augustus.
– Lionel Stevenson

Hand carved column capitals, St. Patricks Roman Catholic Church, Fort Augustus.
– Lionel Stevenson

the roof bosses and column capitals are a beautiful complement to the colour scheme, and the slender column clusters are finely proportioned.

The present church at Fort Augustus replaces an earlier church begun in 1837 by Irish immigrants, but never finished. A second brick church, designed in the neo-Gothic style by John Corbett, was completed in 1870. It suffered a disastrous fire in 1897 that left only the shell of the nave intact. The day after the fire, the Reverend A.J. MacDonald engaged architect William Harris to begin work on its reconstruction, and a week later the plans for it had been completed. The rebuilding, by Lowe Brothers of Charlottetown, took five years to finish, but the September 2, 1903 issue of the *Charlottetown Examiner* called it "the grandest object on a splendid landscape"

Harris added transepts and a circular apse with a row of small lancet windows set high on its wall. These elements were signs of the emerging French Gothic Revival Style in Harris' work. The freize details of the church and presbytery (the latter built around 1875 during the pastorate of Father Angus McDonald) are eye-catching examples of the mason's craft. It is unfortunate that the original spire was not rebuilt atop the church's tower. The spire was removed when it required repairs, and was replaced by the present pyramidal cap which does not enhance the tower's proportions. Nonetheless, St. Patrick's is a well-proportioned church, despite the lack of a clerestory. The interior is certainly one of William Harris' finest.

(see also back cover, page 42)

St. John the Baptist Roman Catholic Church
Miscouche

The eighty-five-foot twin spires of St. John the Baptist Roman Catholic Church can be seen from miles away on the various road approaches to Miscouche. On arrival, one finds a splendid High Victorian Gothic Revival building with side aisles, a clerestory and a sacristy on the east end. The main entry is on the west end, with tower entries on the northwest and southwest corners. These entries are beautifully decorated with Gothic transom windows and hood mouldings.

The interior is highlighted by some colourful stained glass windows in the side aisle walls, but the Gothic window over the main entry is of particular beauty. The nave of the church is 50 by 102 feet and can accommodate five hundred people. The pews are quite handsome, finished in ash and walnut. A choir gallery extends along the west end of the church.

Construction of the church was begun in 1890 and it was dedicated in 1892. It replaces an earlier church built in 1823 that was used as a parish hall after the present church was built. François-Xavier Édouard Meloche may well have been the architect of this church. A decorator/architect from Montreal, he designed Immaculate Conception Roman Catholic Church in Palmer Road which was built in 1892, the same year that this church was completed. The two buildings are remarkably similar in the overall massing of the major components and in the articulation of their facades. Reverend John A. MacDonald supervised the construction of the church and also built the nearby presbytery in 1891. The church bells were installed in 1901, the organ between 1901 and 1905 and the Stations of the Cross in 1921. (see also page 23)

St. John the Baptist Roman Catholic Church, Miscouche.
– Lionel Stevenson

All Saints
Roman Catholic Church
Cardigan Bridge

All Saints Roman Catholic Church, Cardigan Bridge.
– Lionel Stevenson

All Saints Roman Catholic Church in Cardigan Bridge was completed and consecrated in 1874, although its interior was finished in stages after that date. The church, built on a lovely rise just north of the Cardigan River, is French Gothic Revival in style. Its decorative cornerboards, eave bracketing, tall Gothic windows and a three-staged, buttressed tower are typical Gothic Revival elements that complement each other well. The stone Marian archway opposite the front door was built in 1954, and the parochial house nearby was moved to its present site from just east of Charlottetown before 1900. Also, the two corner towers were added to the house at this time, and a new section added to the vestry of the church. Within the past twenty-five years there have been substantial renovations to the church. In 1956 the sanctuary was renovated and a confessional and new communion rail built. In 1963 new pews from a church in East Point were installed. The sanctuary contains a rolling pulpit and, although it is no longer used, it is one of the last surviving movable pulpits on the Island.

The highlight of the interior is the beautiful Gothic altar, built concurrently with the church of Italian marble and Nova Scotia freestone. It was designed and built by William P. Lewis, a prolific stonecarver originally from Dumfries, Scotland. In the transepts are two side altars, one dedicated to St. Joseph and the other to the Blessed Virgin Mary. The vestry (35' x 25') was built during the pastorate of Reverend D. MacDonald. The interior is 80 by 35 feet, and the upper galleries provide additional seating for a large parish of essentially Scottish and Irish origin.

A major renovation was completed recently, including the construction of a basement hall and an entrance vestibule off the rear chapel.

All Saints Roman Catholic Church, Cardigan Bridge.
– Lionel Stevenson

(old) St. James Anglican Church, Port Hill. (1841)
– Lionel Stevenson

St. James Anglican Church
Port Hill

The old St. James Anglican Church in Port Hill, or "the Old Shipbuilders Church," as it was known, was built in 1841. It was not the first church in the area, however; a church building on the farm of Hatfield Maynard preceded it. Prior to its construction, services were conducted in private homes by visiting ministers from the parish of St. Eleanor's.

Reverend William Roche was the first rector in the old St. James Church. The building was used regularly until 1885, when the new St. James Church was built. The old

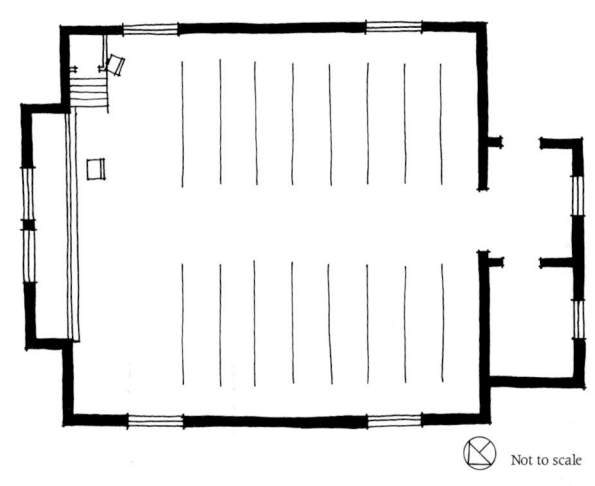

FLOOR PLAN: *(old) St. James Anglican Church, Port Hill.*

Latch detail, (old) St. James Anglican Church, Port Hill.
– Lionel Stevenson

church is now used as a Sunday school, but each summer many tourists are attracted to its simple charm. The fine wood detailing in the vestibule and the old box pews add to its Old World character. At one time the pews were rented to certain families of the congregation, however these rents were later removed and the doors of the pews opened to all.

Approximately twenty by thirty feet, the church sits on a foundation of evenly cut Island sandstone. In 1890 the spire was taken down, and during the First World War, the interior was sheathed and a balcony along the west wall removed. At one time the old church contained a well-stocked library.

The present St. James Anglican Church was built directly across from the old church on Route 12, or the "Ellis River Road," as it is historically known. Although it does not have the detail of St. John's Anglican Church in Ellerslie, it is still a fine structure. "Little" Harry Williams, the renowned builder of the Ellerslie church, was involved in the lowering of the ceiling in 1929.

A stone parsonage was built near the churches in 1852, but it was apparently demolished and replaced by a new rectory in 1877.

St. James United Church, West Covehead — Lionel Stevenson

St. James United Church
West Covehead

One of the earliest Presbyterian congregations of the Island is represented by the neat little church that stands today in a lovely, secluded spot surrounded by trees at the intersection of two roads at West Covehead. The pastoral charge was officially established in Covehead, St. Peter's and Fortune in 1806. As road travel was limited in those days, the first church was built near the Bay shore and later moved a mile inland as more roads were built. In the early 1830s the present church was built, a mile further inland.

Since Reverend James MacGregor first preached in Covehead in 1791, a succession of ministers, most notably the Reverend Messrs. Gordon, Douglass, Allan, and Wilson, has provided continuous service to the community for almost 175 years.

The church has undergone many changes in that period; a major renovation took place shortly after Church Union in 1925. New sills and joists

St. James United Church, West Covehead — Lionel Stevenson

were installed, the roof reshingled and the church repainted inside and out. In the early 1950s the Sunday school rooms were added, electric lights installed and a concrete foundation built. Over the years, the high pulpit has been remodelled and new pews have replaced the early box pews. The hymn singing for many years was led by a precentor, but eventually an organ was purchased. In 1964 the church was again totally repainted and a new floor, ceiling and oil furnace were installed. A small gallery above the front entrance has remained intact. In 1967 the adjacent cemetery was restored, winning first prize in a rural beautification contest.

Although the presence of aluminum doors, electric speaker, window boxes and sign cabinets on the front elevation are somewhat distracting, the church still retains its neo-Classic charm. The simple, symmetrical design, eave returns, corner boards and clapboard siding contribute to its clean and attractive lines. The pedimented front entry, with pilasters, fan light and twin, five-panelled doors is typical of the Classic Revival movement, and its tall, multi-paned Gothic windows help to give the facades both scale and decoration.

Little Sands United Church
Little Sands

Little Sands United Church (formerly Presbyterian) is a peculiar little church on the south shore of King's County. Its angular front elevation is an indigenous style, being an interpretation by local builders of other concurrent trends in religious architecture, the neo-Classic and Carpenter-Gothic styles. The multi-gabled front verandah, alternating vertical and horizontal clapboard siding and small rectangular windows give the front facade a texture, warmth and restrained humour that is not often found in other Island churches. The symbolism of the circular window high in the front of the nave remains somewhat uncertain, although a local authority claims that the twin triangles represent the Double Trinity.

The residents of Little Sands and Wood Islands initially formed one congregation of the Church of Scotland, and the church building they shared was a small (24' x 30'), half-finished hall in Wood Islands. From 1843, Little Sands and Wood Islands were supplied with ministers and probationers of the Free Church of Scotland. During the term of pastor Donald MacNeil (1857-1872), a new church was built at Little Sands and a manse and church were constructed at Wood Islands. In 1892 the Presbytery of Prince Edward Island placed Little Sands with Murray Harbour and Murray River to form a new pastoral charge. In 1898 the present church at little Sands was built under the direction of D.J. MacLean.

Little Sands United Church – Lionel Stevenson

Although the interior has been modernized, the old box pews remain. When Church Union came into effect, in 1925, Little Sands became part of the United Church of Canada.

Little Sands United Church is located on Route 4, overlooking Northumberland Strait.

St. John's Anglican Church
Milton

St. John's Anglican Church, built in 1898, replaces an earlier church built in 1841. Typical of architect William Harris' later and smaller Prince Edward Island churches, it is a pretty little church built on the crest of one of the Island's long, rolling hills, on Route 2 at Milton in Queen's County. The structure is significant because it is the first of Harris' small churches (typically built for Anglican congregations) to be designed in the French Gothic Revival style, with an apsidal chancel and asymmetrically located tower and spire. St. John's is also the only one of Harris' post-1895 churches still painted exactly according to his specifications: grey with white trim, and brown facing on the tower. The interior is dominated by a groin-vaulted ceiling in stained spruce that extends over the entire width of the nave, without the aid of intermediate support from arcade piers. Three lancet windows are later additions to the chancel, which Harris originally intended to be indirectly lit by the large traceried window in the transept gable. These windows not only provide more light in the chancel, but also help reduce the lowering horizontality of the entire church.

St. John's Anglican Church, Milton. — Lionel Stevenson

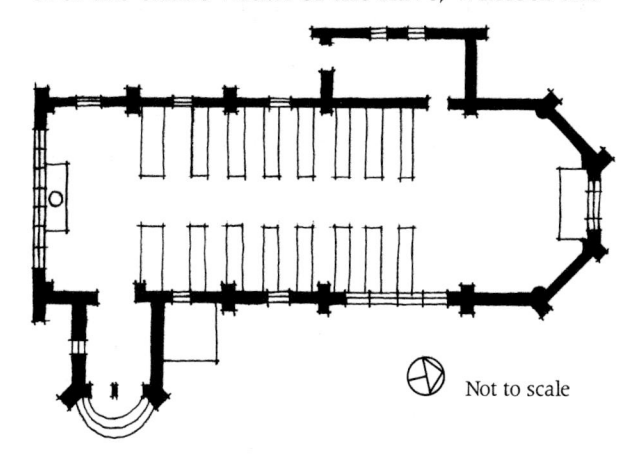

FLOOR PLAN: *St. John's Anglican Church, Milton.*

St. John's Anglican Church, St. Eleanor's. — Lionel Stevenson

St. John's Anglican Church
St. Eleanor's

The first St. John's Church was built in 1825-1828 in the parish of Richmond, the second Anglican parish to be established in the colony. It was destroyed by fire in 1835 but a second church, practically a replica of the first, was built in 1838-1842. Both churches were built by George Tanton, a prolific and highly skilled builder in the area and although recent renovations have masked much of his detailing, the building has still retained the refined appeal of a neo-Gothic English parish church. It is a well proportioned building with a three stage, buttressed tower topped with a battlemented parapet, crocketed pinnacles and an octagonal spire. A chancel was added to the east end of the church in 1888 and in 1967 a lych gate was erected as a Centennial project. The interior has some fine stained glass but the highlight is really the cabinetry of Robert Ellis. The pine gallery facing is particularly attractive.

St. Martin's Roman Catholic Church
Cumberland

St. Martin's Roman Catholic Church is located on the south shore of Queen's County, overlooking Northumberland Strait. According to parish history, it was originally intended to be built of wood, but became instead one of the smallest stone churches in eastern Canada. Indeed, the rural sandstone church is rare on the Island. Begun in 1867 on land donated by Patrick Scott, it was built of sandstone quarried at Matthew Murphy's farm nearby. The church was completed in 1868. An interesting detail is the framing of the nave windows in brick, an attractive and practical masonry technique. The tower and top half of the front gable on the north facade are also built of brick, but the church was built of stone for fire protection — a good idea considering the casualty rate among Island churches at the time. It has also withstood the rather severe winters on the Strait for 116

St. Martin's Roman Catholic Church, Cumberland. – Scott Smith

years, another good indicator that Island sandstone is a lot more durable than some have thought.

The church (60' x 26') was built by Lawrence and Peter Murphy under the supervision of architect John Corbett. In 1971, the brick vestry was rebuilt in wood and the church bell was installed

Cross Roads Christian Church (formerly First Baptist Church)
Cross Roads

Cross Roads Christian Church (c. 1980) — Lionel Stevenson

The Church at Cross Roads, just to the east of Charlottetown, was founded in 1810 by John R. Stewart, an immigrant from Perthshire, Scotland. The early members were "Scotch" Baptists, influenced by the Haldane movement in Scotland, but not officially members of the Baptist church. Alexander Crawford was the first consecrated preacher in this fledgling community, arriving on the Island in 1815 from Yarmouth, Nova Scotia. The first meeting house was built in 1813; it was a small (30' x 20') log building "without plaster, pews, pulpit or gallery or anything to mark it as a House of Prayer." Construction of the present church commenced in 1836, and in 1839 the old hall was torn down. In 1844, during the pastorate of the Reverend Dr. John Knox, a Mission house, or manse, was begun. It was finished in 1846. In 1877 the cemetery was planned, and by the turn of the century, the church had lost many of its members through deaths, people moving, and a schism within the Church.

In 1925 the church was rededicated, and it became known as Cross Roads Christian Church. Extensive repairs were made to the building at this time, and the interior, with its plain vertical wood siding, was completely renovated. This building originally had square-headed windows and some of the upper windows had been removed, but an extensive renovation in 1988 restored them. A complete basement and two-story front vestibule were added and the interior was extensively renovated. Under the direction of Donald F. Stewart and with help of many volunteers, the church was officially re-opened for regular services on August 7, 1988, for the first time since 1972.

Princetown United Church
Malpeque

One of the finest examples of Carpenter-Gothic church architecture on the Island is this church in Malpeque, built in 1869-1870. It replaces an earlier log building that was perhaps the earliest Presbyterian church in Prince Edward Island, built around 1794 at Ellison's Brook. It was moved on skids to the site of the present church in 1810. In this same year, a second church — more of a meeting house — was begun. It was completed in 1813 and the tiny log church was consequently used as a school and Small Debts Court. The minister of this second church was the Reverend Dr. John Keir, a prominent figure in Malpeque's history and the first Protestant minister ordained on the Island.

Princetown United Church, Malpeque. — Scott Smith

An article in the October 25, 1870, issue of the semi-weekly *Charlottetown Patriot* described the new (third) church:

The church which is tastefully designed and neatly finished is 75 feet long by 50 feet wide, and will seat 800 persons. The height of the post is 25 feet and the

Reverend Dr. John Keir.
– Public Archives Prince Edward Island

Princetown United Church, Malpeque, early 1900s.
– Public Archives Prince Edward Island

total height of the tower and spire about 111 feet. Windows are of the Gothic style. The internal arrangements of the building are neat and comfortable. There is an end gallery, and the pews and pulpit are of the modern style. An arched recess behind the pulpit has a fine effect besides relieving the darkness of the windowless wall. Altogether it is a handsome church and reflects great credit upon the Princetown congregation, who have built it at a cost of $1800.

Renovations to the interior, particularly in 1976, have been extensive but the most significant acquisition was the splendid pipe organ obtained in 1918 from the old Grace Methodist Church in Charlottetown. Although the steeple was damaged by lightning in 1925 and a section of the tower torn down in 1960, the building still emphasized verticality in the Gothic Revival tradition. When the spire was reconstructed in 1984 the church was returned to its original form and this verticality accentuated even further. The corner finials, sculpted vergeboard and lancet windows combine to give the front facade a highly chiselled appearance. The narrow bands of shingling give the elevations a textured surface but at the same time do not detract from the overall vertical thrust.

Controversy continues to surround the origin, ownership and whereabouts of the church bell. The Acadian community and the United Church both claim the bell, but it has been stolen twice and remains missing. *(see also page 24)*

East Point United Baptist Church — Lionel Stevenson

East Point United Baptist Church
East Point

This intricate pattern of shingles can be seen above the front nave window on East Point United Baptist Church, at the extreme eastern tip of the Island. The present church was built in 1903, in the Akron plan, a church style that was favoured by Baptists and Methodists for their post-1870 church buildings throughout North America. It was the third church that the Kingsboro Baptists had erected on that site. A meeting house (1833) and a larger church with a tall spire (1864) preceded it.

(see also page 30)

St. Mark's Anglican Church, Kensington   – Scott Smith

St. Mark's Anglican Church
Kensington

St. Mark's Anglican in Kensington was one of the first church commissions on Prince Edward Island for noted architect William Critchlow Harris, succeeding only Tryon (Methodist) United (see p. 119).

Built in 1885 in the English Gothic Revival style, St. Mark's is one of the few remaining board-and-batten church buildings in PEI, and indeed the Maritimes. It is delightfully proportioned, with its low profile dominated by a three-stage corner steeple and octagonal spire, a Harris characteristic early in his career. Groupings of lancet windows with Tudor hood mouldings, divided by false buttresses, surround the nave and tower.

The interior is highlighted by a decorative arcade in the east wall of the chancel and a hand-grained pulpit.

In 1992-94 St. Mark's was substantially restored, including the removal of an obtrusive chimney from its front facade and the reinstatement of its original colour scheme. The building was moved 12 feet away from the adjacent road and set on a new concrete foundation. The basement created houses a badly needed hall, kitchen and washrooms. The interior was also repainted, mostly in pastels. For their significant restoration effort, St. Mark's was awarded a Preservation Award from the PEI Museum and Heritage Foundation in June, 1994.

St. Mark's Anglican Church, Kensington – Scott Smith

Immaculate Conception Roman Catholic Church
PalmerRoad

When the first mission church in Palmer Road parish burned to the ground in 1890, the parishioners and clergy decided almost immediately to build anew. Their parish of approximately 600 families, mostly of Acadian and Irish descent, had been experiencing significant social and economic growth.

The new church that they built was an imposing structure – the largest wood frame church on the Island, seating 1000 people. Built in 1891-93 by Dunstan Martin, who was also building a similar church in Miscouche (see p. 93), Immaculate Conception was designed by a Montreal architect/decorator, François-Xavier Édouard Meloche (see p. 68-70) in the French Gothic Revival style, so common in the High Victorian period.

Creating an integrated interior design for such a large church was a challenge well met by Meloche. The soaring, exposed trusses, with their pointed Gothic arches, dominate the nave and the lower nave windows contain a complete cycle of modern stained glass, designed and built in the 1980s by John Burden and Blaine Hrabi. The magnificent Rose Window over the front entrance was built in Newcastle, N.B. and brought by schooner to nearby Miminegash harbour. The paintings of the Stations of the Cross, although unsigned, were probably executed in Meloche's

Entrance, Immaculate Conception Roman Catholic Church, Palmer Road – Scott Smith

Montreal studio. The highly ornate altars, designed and built by the prolific Bernard Creamer of Souris, were installed in the sanctuary in 1903. A rare Karn reed organ, recently mechanized, was purchased around 1900.

Interior, Immaculate Conception Roman Catholic Church, Palmer Road   – Scott Smith

The exterior is dominated by the asymmetric front (north) facade containing the Rose Window. The detailing around the front entrance – a steep gabled roof and inticate shingle pattern – are a concession to the increasing flamboyance in the expression of High Victorianism. The corner steeples are quite different. The taller is pure Gothic while the shorter one, without a spire, is more Baroque in style. The latter contains an impressive statue of the Virgin Mary in its niche.

Almost 8 feet tall and weighing 1800 pounds, the statue was dedicated, with much fanfare, concurrently with the dedication of the church in 1893. Bishop MacDonald of Charlottetown attended and called the church "a masterpiece of its kind".

111

Immaculate Conception Roman Catholic Church, Palmer Road – Scott Smith

St. Andrew's Chapel — Scott Smith

St. Andrew's Chapel

St. Andrew's Chapel literally rose from the ashes of a devastating fire in Charlottetown in 1987 to be relocated to its original site 30 kilometers up the Hillsborough River, where it was completely rebuilt in 1990.

The story of its resurrection is very compelling and a testament not only to the forethought of Bishop Angus Bernard McEachern, who built such a substantial building in the first place, in 1804-05, but to the Diocese, parishioners, historians and The Friends of St. Andrew's who found the will, the funds and the energy to make this project a reality.

Replaced by a larger church in St. Andrew's in 1862, the Chapel was hauled on the ice down the Hillsborough River in 1864 – a Herculean, dangerous, three-day effort of men and several teams of horses – and landed in Charlottetown. It served as a convent for the Sisters of Notre Dame for over 100 years. Abandoned and threatened with demolition after the fire of 1987, the building was cut into four sections, hauled to St. Andrew's on a flat bed truck and rebuilt on a new concrete foundation. The hefty, hand-hewn structural frame and exterior wide board sheathing survived the fire and these two arduous moves. New exterior shingling, interior cladding and flooring were applied in 1990. The locations of the original round-headed

Interior, St. Andrew's Chapel — Scott Smith

Georgian windows were fortuitously discovered during the reconstruction.

The interior of the rebuilt Chapel and added rear vestry is quite warm, clad entirely in horizontal pine. Ornamentation is minimal and the original frame is exposed in appropriate places. The simple altar, bench pews and railings contribute to the elegantly refined interior – inviting and comfortable.

St. Andrew's Chapel is a fine example of the dignified and stately proportions reflecting the order of the neo-Classical style. Its eave returns, fan light over the front entrance and round-headed windows are distinctly Georgian. It sits in a quiet grove of trees just off the main highway to Charlottetown and is now used year-round for lectures, concerts, family reunions and anniversary celebrations.

The Friends of St. Andrew's received Heritage awards from the PEI Museum and Heritage Foundation in 1998 and 1999.

St. Joachim's Roman Catholic Church, Vernon River
– Scott Smith

St. Joachim's Roman Catholic Church
Vernon River

St. Joachim's is the fourth Roman Catholic church building to be constructed since 1804 in Vernon River, a large parish of Scottish and Irish settlement just east of Charlottetown. On an elevated site, it has long been a landmark for woodsmen and travellers in the area.

Due to a desire to make church buildings more fireproof and a subsequent proliferation of brick kilns on the Island, St. Joachim's was one of several churches that were built of Island-made brick in the latter half of the nineteenth century. The design of this large (125' x 62') Gothic Revival building has been attributed to architect John McLellan, an Island native who also designed St.

1880 drawing of St. Joachim's Roman Catholic Church, Vernon River, showing original spire and parochial house.

Joseph's Convent in Charlottetown and St. Brigid's, Foxley River (1873). Construction began in 1877 and the church was consecrated and formally opened, with great ceremony, in 1879.

Built at a cost of over $30,000, St. Joachim's is a very substantial building. Set on a stone foundation, the red brick is very high quality and quite hard. Unfortunately, the original spire, which rose majestically on its steeple to a height of 150 ft., has been truncated by decay and a lightning strike. Despite this loss, the building still exhibits great proportion, as does the brick parochial house (1868) nearby.

The interior features a groined ceiling, some lovely stained glass and a vestry and side chapel off the nave. The ornate Gothic altar, standing over 22 ft. tall, was built by John Newson and painted by John Murphy, both of Charlottetown. A bell was installed in 1886 and a parish hall built across the road in 1900. In 1902, the elegant pipe organ was installed in the choir loft.

Interior, St. Joachim's Roman Catholic Church, Vernon River   – Scott Smith

St. Peter's United Church
St. Peter's Bay

Built in 1886 for a Presbyterian congregation, St. Peter's United is a delightful Gothic Revival building. Its highly articulated three-stage steeple has a lovely spire and Wren-like proportions.

St. Peter's United Church, St. Peter's Bay – Lionel Stevenson

Tryon United Church   – Scott Smith

Tryon United Church

Tryon United was one of the first large church commissions for renowned Island architect W.C. Harris. It was built in 1881 for a Methodist congregation, succeeding an early meeting house (1817) and a chapel built in 1839. Despite some square-headed nave windows, Tryon United was cited by the National Historic Sites and Monuments Board in 1992 as an "exceptional example of High Victorian Gothic Revival style...". Its picturesque corner tower is indeed a landmark in the Tryon area. The wife of Surveyor General Samuel Holland is buried in the adjacent Peoples' Cemetery.

St. Francis de Sales Roman Catholic Church
Little Pond

This tidy little church was built in 1863 to serve its Scottish and Acadian parishioners, who unfortunately never enjoyed the company of a full time pastor. With its Gothic tracery, clean, elegant lines and distinctive spire, it sits on a pretty lot in Little Pond.

St. Francis de Sales Roman Catholic Church, Little Pond
– Scott Smith

St. Ann's Roman Catholic Church
Lennox Island

Most of PEI's native Mi'kmaq population converted to Roman Catholicism and began a migration to Lennox Island in the early 19th century. This handsome Gothic-style church was designed by Summerside architect George Baker. It was built in 1895, replacing a frame building (1842) destroyed by fire.

St. Ann's Roman Catholic Church, Lennox Island
– Scott Smith

Glossary

apse: a semicircular or polygonal recess in a church, terminating an axis and intended to house an altar. **Apsidal**: pertaining to an apse or similar to one.

arcade: a covered walk with a line of counterthrusting arches raised on columns or piers along one or both long sides.

buttress: an exterior mass of masonry set at an angle or bonded to a wall to absorb lateral thrusts from roof vaults. **Sham buttress**: a buttress as a decorative element, usually in a wooden frame. **Flying buttress**: a bar of masonry connecting a vault to a pier or buttress below; a distinctly Gothic feature.

bell tower (campanile): a tall structure, either independent or part of a building, to contain one or more bells.

bellcast: a roof or eave with a flared edge, shaped like a bell.

boss: a projecting, carved ornament placed at the intersection of ribs, groins, etc. or at the termination of a moulding.

broached spire: an octagonal spire rising without a parapet above a tower, with pyramidal forms at the angles of the tower.

brick nogging: brick laid in the spaces between timber in a wood-frame partition.

board and batten: a wall covering constructed of broad vertical boards whose joints are covered by narrow vertical strips of wood.

capital: the topmost member, usually decorative, of a column or pilaster.

chancel: the space reserved for clergy and choir.

clerestory: upper stage in a building, pierced with windows that admit light to the centre of a lofty room.

colombage bousillée: timber frame filled with a mixture of clay and straw and held in place by struts or waffles between upright members.

cornice: an ornamental projecting moulding along the top of a wall or building; the uppermost division of an entablature.

corner board: a board which is used as trim on the external corner of a wood-frame structure and against which the ends of the siding are fitted.

dormer: a window projecting from a sloping roof.

eave returns: the continuation of an eave line in a different direction, usually at a right angle.

entablature: the elaborated beam member carried by classical columns.

fenestration: the architectural arrangement of windows and other openings in the walls of a building.

finial: an ornament at the top of a roof or decorating the top of any item, such as a tower corner or a pew.

flèches: a slender wooden spire arising from a roof; a distinctly Gothic feature.

fresco: a mural painted into fresh lime plaster.

freize: a decorative band in a stringcourse, below the cornice; the middle horizontal member of a classical entablature.

façade: the exterior face which is the architectural front of the building.

frow (froe): a wedge-like tool used with a mallet to split timber into boards or shingles. *(see also page 31)*

freestone: any stone, such as sandstone or limestone, that can be cut in any direction without breaking.

gabled roof: a roof having a gable (triangular portions of vertical wall) at one or both ends.

gallery: an elevated section of the seating area of a church, sometimes set apart for special uses.

grisaille: a system of painting in grey tints of various shades for decoration or to represent objects in relief.

groin vault: a compound vault in which barrel vaults intersect.

hipped roof: a roof which slopes upward from all four sides of a building.

hood moulding: the projecting moulding of the arch over a door or window; also called a dripstone.

indigenous: originating or occurring naturally in the place specified.

lancet: a narrow window with a sharp pointed arch typical of English Gothic.

label: a square-arched dripstone or hood mould.

lantern: a windowed superstructure crowning a roof or dome.

Lady Chapel: chapel dedicated to the Virgin Mary and often located at the eastern end of a church behind the high altar.

Marian arch: arch dedicated to the Virgin Mary.

mortise and tenon: a joint made by fitting a piece of wood with a projection (tenon) into a slot (mortise) in another piece of wood.

moulding: a shaped strip of wood, often placed around the upper walls of rooms. Usually ornamental, it often conceals joints.

nave: the main portion of a church, where the congregation is seated.

niche: a recess in a wall for a statue or other object.

pediment: the broad triangular end of a gable, or a triangular element resembling it, on the front of a building.

pilaster: a decorative column applied to a wall.

parquet: inlaid wood flooring, usually set in simple geometric patterns.

parapet: a low wall at the edge of a platform or above the roof gutter.

pièces sur pièces: a form of wooden construction in which the walls of a framed building are made of horizontal, squared timbers.

piquet: round post used in vertical timber wall construction.

quoins: cornerstones or blocks forming an outside angle at the junction of two walls.

quatrefoil: panel divided by cusps (triangular projections) into four sections.

reredos: screen or ornamental wall rising behind an altar.

rib-vault: a vault in which the ribs support, or seem to support, the web of the vault.

rosette: a round pattern with a carved or painted conventionalized floral motif.

rose window: a large, circular medieval window containing tracery disposed in a radial manner.

sanctuary: the portion of a church containing the altar.

sacristy: a room in or adjoining a church where the vestments, sacred vessels, etc. are kept.

side-aisle: one of the corridors running parallel to the nave of a church and separated from it by an arcade or colonnade.

ship's knees: an ell-shaped timber used to reinforce the joint between the major structural members of a timber frame.

spire: a tall pyramidal, polygonal or conical structure rising above a tower and terminating in a point.

tracery: ornamental intersecting work in the head or top of a window.

transept: transverse arms of a cruciform or cross-shaped church.

transom window: a window above a doorway.

transverse axis: the axis at right angles to the longitudinal axis of a church.

truncated: shortened or cut off to a square or blunt end.

turret: a diminutive tower, characteristically corbeled from a corner.

vergeboard (bargeboard): sloping, decorative board along edge of gable roof covering the roof timbers.

vestry (sacristy): a room for the storage of vestments and altar clothes.

wainscoting: a decorative or protective facing applied to the lower portion of an interior partition or wall.

window sash (12/8): the number of panes in the upper sash relative to the number of panes in the lower sash of a double-hung window.

Period Styles

Romanesque: The style emerging in Western Europe in the early eleventh century based on Roman and Byzantine elements; characterized by massive articulated wall structures, round arches and powerful vaults.

Norman: The Romanesque architecture of England, from the Norman Conquest (1066) until the rise of the Gothic (1180).

Gothic: The architectural style of the High Middle Ages in Western Europe. It emerged from Romanesque and Byzantine forms in France during the late twelfth century. Its great works are cathedrals characterized by the pointed arch, the rib vault, the development of the exterior flying buttress and the gradual reduction of the walls to a system of richly decorated fenestration.

Decorated Phase: The second of the three phases of English Gothic architecture from circa 1280 to after 1350. Characterized by rich decoration and tracery, multiple ribs and ogee arches.

Perpendicular Phase: The last and longest phase of Gothic architecture in England, circa 1350-1550. Characterized by vertical emphasis in structure and elaborate fan vaults.

Tudor: The final development of English Perpendicular Gothic architecture in the period 1485-1547; characterized by four-centered arches.

Palladianism: A mode of building following the strict Roman forms, as set forth in the publications of the Italian Renaissance architect Andrea Palladio (1508-1580); applied in England in the eighteenth century.

Georgian: The prevailing style of the eighteenth century in Great Britain and in North America from 1714-1820. Derived from classical, Palladian, Renaissance and Baroque forms. Named after George I, George II and George III.

Classical Revival: An architectural movement based on the use of pure Roman and Greek forms, mainly in England and the United States, in the early nineteenth century.

neo-Gothic, neo-Classic: Refers to the use of Gothic or Classical forms during the Gothic or Classical Revivals.

Gothic Revival: A movement originating in the eighteenth and culminating in the nineteenth century, flourishing throughout Europe and the United States, which aimed at reviving the spirit and forms of Gothic architecture.

High Victorian Gothic Revival: The most picturesque and flamboyant period of the Gothic Revival, from 1860-1890. Named after Queen Victoria.

Carpenter-Gothic: In nineteenth-century North America, the application of Gothic motifs, often elaborate, by artisan-builders in wood.

Picturesque: A highly decorated and quaint interpretation of the Gothic Revival in the period 1850-1870, with an emphasis on landscaping, asymmetry and "movement."

Italianate: The eclectic form fashionable in England and the United States in the 1840s and 1850s; characterized by low-pitched, heavily bracketed roofs, asymmetrical plan, square towers and round-arched windows.

Spanish Revival: An American Revival in the early 1900s featuring decorated curvilinear window surrounds, cornices and parapets.

Château: In the late nineteenth century in North America, a massive and irregular style characterized by steeply pitched hip roofs and round towers with conical roofs.

Vernacular: A mode of building based on regional forms and materials.

Selected Bibliography

Butchart, Reuben. *History of the Disciples of Christ in Canada Since 1830*, Canadian Headquarters Publication, Church of Christ (Disciples), 1949.

Cran, Emily. *A Brief History of the Parish of Saint Simon and Saint Jude, Tignish, P.E.I.* Liturgical Committee, 1970.

Crowdis, C.J. *History of the Princetown United Church.* Halifax: 1958.

Ford, Reverend John A. and Reverend Henry G. Mellick. *Historical Sketch of the East Point Baptist Church*, Centennial, July 1833-July 1933.

Hickey, Kathleen. *Facts of Saint Mary's Church, Indian River, P.E.I. From Beginning to Present.*

History of Covehead Church. 1969.

History of the Indian River. W.I.I.R., Centennial Project, 1973.

l'Impartial Illustre, History of Tignish from 1799. 1899 Centennial Issue, published in magazine form.

Johnstone, William E. *The Life of Dr. John and Mrs. Geddie* and *Early Presbyterian History, 1770-1845.* New London, P.E.I.: Geddie Memorial Church, 1975.

Langford, Brendan. "A Study of Saint Mary's Roman Catholic Church at Indian River." Halifax: NSCAD, unpublished.

MacDougall, Arlene and Violet MacEachern. *The Banks of the Elliot.* Charlottetown: Irwin, 1973.

MacLennan, Jean. *From Shore to Shore.* Edinburgh: Knox Press, 1977.

MacLeod, Rev. John. *History of Presbyterianism on P.E.I.* Chicago: Winona, 1904.

MacNeill, M.A. *A History of the United Churches of Murray Harbour, Murray River and Little Sands, 1815-1965.*

MacQueen, Malcolm. *Skye Pioneers and "The Island".* Winnipeg: Stroud, 1929.

McCallum, Lena. *A Historical Sketch of the Christian Church at Cross Roads, 1810-1961.*

Malpeque and its People (1700-1982), Malpeque Historical Society. Summerside: 1982.

Martin, Finley. *A View From The Bridge.* Montague: 1984.

Mellish, John T. *Outlines of the History of Methodism in Charlottetown, P.E.I.* Charlottetown: Haszard, 1888.

Millman, T.R. *History of the Parish of New London.* Toronto: 1949.

Millman, T.R. *History of Port Hill Parish.* Toronto: 1949.

Putnam, Ada Macleod. *The Selkirk Settlers and the Church They Built at Belfast.* Toronto: Presbyterian Publications, 1939.

Ross, Matilde and Sadie Jones. *Pioneer Builder of Saint John's Church, Historic Sidelights.* Charlottetown: P.E.I. Historical Society, 1956.

Sinnott, F.H. *A History of the Baptists of P.E.I.* Liverpool, N.S.: K&W Enterprises, 1973.

Wallace, William. *250 Years Young, Our Diocesan Story, 1710-1960*, pp. 107-120.

Weale, David. "The Time is Come! Millenarianism in Colonial P.E.I." *Acadiensis*, Vol. 7. Autumn, 1977. pp. 35-48.

Weale, David."'The Minister': The Reverend Donald McDonald." *The Island Magazine*, No. 3. Fall-Winter, 1977, pp. 1-6.

The author acknowledges reference to various church records and histories, parish histories and the mission histories and Diocesan files of the Roman Catholic Church.

Articles from the following newspapers were also consulted: *The Examiner*, the Charlottetown *Guardian-Patriot*, *The Islander*, the Charlottetown *Herald*, *The P.E.I. Register* and the *Journal-Pioneer*. The Centennial Edition (1973) of the *Guardian-Patriot* was a main source of information. The author has specific information on these references, if required.

General Bibliography

Anson, Peter F. *Fashions in Church Furnishings*. London: Studio Vista, 1965.

Blanchard, J.-Henri. *Histoire des Acadiens de l'Isle de Prince Edouard*. Summerside: 1975.

Bowyer, Jack. *The Evolution of Church Building*. London: Granada, 1977.

Bremner, Benjamin. *An Island Scrapbook*. Charlottetown: Irwin, 1932.

Brosseau, Mathilde. "Gothic Revival in Canadian Architecture." Canadian Historic Sites, Occasional Papers, No. 25.

Cullen, Mary. "Pre-1755 Acadian Building Techniques." Agenda Paper, Parks Canada.

Clark, A.H. *Three Centuries and the Island*. Toronto: University of Toronto Press, 1959.

Duffus, Allan, Edward MacFarlane, Elizabeth Pacey and George Rogers. *Thy Dwellings Fair*. Hantsport, N.S.: Lancelot, 1982.

Dupont, J.-Claude. *Histoire Populaire de l'Acadie*. Montreal: Lemeac, 1978.

Gowans, Alan. *Building Canada*. Toronto: Oxford, 1966.

Hamilton, William. *Local History in Atlantic Canada*. Toronto: Macmillan, 1974.

Harris, Cyril M. *Historic Architecture Sourcebook*. New York: McGraw-Hill, 1977.

Hennessey, Michael F. *The Catholic Church in P.E.I.* Charlottetown: Roman Catholic Episcopal Corporation, 1979.

Kalman, H. and J. deVisser. *Pioneer Churches*. Toronto: McClelland and Stewart, 1976.

Lucas, Glenn. "Canadian Protestant Church History to 1973." *The Bulletin*, No. 23, 1974. Toronto: United Church Publishing House, 1974

MacFadyen, Jean. *For the Sake of the Record*. Summerside: Private, l980. pp. 21-86.

MacRae, Marion. *Hallowed Walls*. Toronto: Clarke-Irwin, 1975.

Meachem, J.H. and Co. *Illustrated Historical Atlas of P.E.I. 1880*. Charlottetown: Centennial Edition, 1973.

Ondaatje, Kim. *Small Churches of Canada*. Toronto: Lester and Orpen Denys Ltd., 1982.

Pacey, Elizabeth, George Rogers and Allan Duffus. *More Stately Mansions*. Hantsport, N.S.: Lancelot, 1983.

Ross, Leone M. "Houses of Worship." *Canadian Collector*, P.E.I. Centenary Issue, 1973. pp. 36-39.

Stanton, Phoebe. *The Gothic Revival and American Church Architecture: An Episode in Taste*. Baltimore: The Johns Hopkins University Press, 1968.

Sharpe, Errol. *A People's History of Prince Edward Island*. Toronto: Steel Rail Publishing, 1976.

Tuck, Robert C. *Gothic Dreams*. Toronto: Dundurn, 1978.

Tuck, Robert C. "William Harris and His Island Churches." *The Island Magazine*, No. 2. Spring-Summer 1977.

Warburton, A.B. *A History of Prince Edward Island*. Saint John: Barnes, 1923.

West, G.H. *Gothic Architecture in England and France*. London: Bell and Sons, 1927.

– Christine Callaghan

About the Author

Scott Smith is an architect and journalist with a practice in Halifax, Nova Scotia. Born in Montreal, Quebec, he received a Bachelor of Science degree from Mount Allison University in 1967, and a Bachelor of Architecture degree from the School of Architecture, Technical University of Nova Scotia, in 1972. He lived and worked in Charlottetown from 1978 to 1981, during which period he conducted research for this, his first book.

An active conservationist, he has developed a system for recording and evaluating historic buildings. He has lectured on Prince Edward Island architecture at the 1980 Atlantic Canada Institute Conference at the University of Prince Edward Island, conducted a photo survey of historic buildings in Colchester County, Nova Scotia, and his photographs have appeared in many architectural publications. His articles on architectural history have been published by such periodicals as *Arts Atlantic* (Spring 1985) and *Canadian Antiques and Art Review* (September 1981), and he has written book reviews for *The Island* Magazine and *The Atlantic Provinces Book Review*.

Index of Churches

Acadian chapel, Mt. Carmel 15
All Saints Cathedral, Halifax, N.S. 27
All Saints R.C., Cardigan Bridge 94
All Soul's Chapel, Charlottetown 27, 42, 45, 76
Alma United Baptist 46
Barrington Meeting House, Barrington, N.S. 18
Cascumpec United 25
Central Christian Church, Charlottetown 25
Christ Church Anglican, Kildare Capes 51
Christ Church Cathedral, Fredericton, N.B. 21, 22
Church of Christ, Montague 25, 32, 57
Church of Notre Dame, Montreal, Que. 21
Cross Roads Christian 19, 104
East Point United Baptist 30, 107
Free Church of Scotland, Desable 19, 46, 78
Geddie Memorial, Springbrook 19, 32, 37, 46, 71
Hartsville Presbyterian 43
Holy Trinity Anglican, Georgetown 46, 58
Immaculate Conception R.C., Brae 41, 42
Immaculate Conception R.C., Palmer Road 110
Little Sands United 25, 100
Marylbone Chapel, London, England 17
New Glasgow United 3
Notre Dame de Mont Carmel R.C. 32, 34
Orwell Corner United 48
Princetown United, Malpeque 24, 105
Sacred Heart R.C., Mount Ryan 25, 56
St. Andrew's Chapel 113
St. Anne's Chapel, Fredericton, N.B. 21
St. Ann's R.C., Lennox Island 120
St. Augustine's R.C., South Rustico 12, 23, 82
St. Bonaventure's R.C., Tracadie Cross 36, 84
St. Brigid's R.C., Foxley River 116
St. Dunstan's Basilica, Charlottetown 23, 33, 44, 52, 53

St. Elizabeth's Anglican, Springfield 27
St. Francis de Sales R.C., Little Pond 120
St. James Anglican, Port Hill 96
St. James R.C., Summerfield 25
St. James United, West Covehead 19, 20, 98
St. Joachim's R.C., Vernon River 32, 115
St. John's Anglican, Ellerslie 6, 24, 25, 35, 39, 80
St. John's Anglican, Milton 24, 27, 101
St. John's Anglican, St. Eleanor's 17, 102
St. John's Anglican, Saint John, N.B. 21
St. John the Baptist Cathedral, St. John's NF 21
St. John the Baptist R.C., Miscouche 23, 93
St. John's Presbyterian, Belfast 25, 26, 32, 35, 40, 63
St. John's United, Mount Stewart 33
St. Malachy's R.C., Kinkora 28
St. Mark's Anglican, Kensington 31, 108
St. Martin's R.C., Cumberland 32, 103
St. Mary's Anglican, Snettisham, England 21
St. Mary's Anglican, Summerside 24
St. Mary's R.C., Indian River 24, 28, 29, 34, 35, 38, 42, 47, 59, front cover
St. Mary's R.C., Souris 33, 34, 89
St. Patrick's R.C., Fort Augustus 27, 32, 42, 91, back cover
St. Patrick's R.C., Grand River 55
St. Paul's Anglican, Charlottetown 13, 24, 27, 38, 74
St. Paul's Anglican, Halifax, N.S. 17
St. Paul's R.C., Sturgeon 33, 45, 87
St. Peter's Cathedral, Charlottetown 24
St. Peter's United, St. Peter's Bay 118
St. Simon and St. Jude R.C., Tignish 23, 24, 32, 67
St. Thomas's Anglican, Long Creek 27
South Winsloe United 32, 54
Tryon United 119
Victoria United 14